John Emery Morris

The Resseguie family.

A historical and genealogical record of Alexander Resseguie of Norwalk, Conn., and

four generations of his descendants

John Emery Morris

The Resseguie family.
A historical and genealogical record of Alexander Resseguie of Norwalk, Conn., and four generations of his descendants

ISBN/EAN: 9783337724337

Printed in Europe, USA, Canada, Australia, Japan

Cover: Foto ©ninafisch / pixelio.de

More available books at **www.hansebooks.com**

THE RESSEGUIE FAMILY.

A Historical and Genealogical Record

OF

ALEXANDER RESSEGUIE,

OF NORWALK, CONN.,

AND FOUR GENERATIONS OF HIS DESCENDANTS.

COMPILED BY JOHN E. MORRIS.

HARTFORD, CONN.:
PRESS OF THE CASE, LOCKWOOD & BRAINARD COMPANY.
1888.

INTRODUCTION.

In view of the fact that the advent of the Resseguie family in America occurred nearly a century after the earliest settlements had been made, and at a period when the eastern coast had become comparatively well populated, and when town and church organizations had long been completed, it appears somewhat remarkable that no more of a historical nature can be learned concerning them than at present seems possible. The early family was composed of a sturdy, middle-class people, descendants of the Huguenots and Puritans, in whom, especially in the first two or three generations, the pioneer instinct seems to have been remarkably prominent. The manifest desire to make a way for themselves, a distaste for clannish village civilization, and a deep enjoyment of the life of nature to be met with in the forest clearing, urged them instinctively to push further and further into the wilderness, and left no time nor taste for a record of their lives and deeds; and this may, in a measure, account for the sparse and fragmentary evidence of their history, the loss of which we now so much regret. The full genealogy upon which the compiler has been more or less diligently engaged since 1883, and subscriptions for which have been repeatedly solicited, records over four thousand of the descendants of Alexander Resseguie, in eight generations, and would form a printed book of seven hundred pages. Its abandonment and the substitution of the present little work arise from the complete failure of the many efforts to obtain subscriptions at all approaching the cost of the former; while the latter is offered in order that the attainable facts of the early history may be preserved. The five generations noted herein, while containing but one-seventh of the descendants enumerated in the manuscript genealogy, carry the line of descent so near to the present day that searchers may readily connect themselves with their ancestry.

J. E. M.

DE RESSEGUIER.

ARMS. — RESSEGUIER. — ROUERGUE.

"D'or à l'arbre de sin.; au chef cousu d'arg. ch. de trois roses de gu."
Rietstap, Armorial Général.

A green tree upon a golden shield, a silver chevron having upon it three red roses.

Appearances point chiefly to the province of Languedoc, in Southern France, as the ancient home of the Resseguie family; and to Toulouse, the capital of the department of Haute-Garonne, as their native city. In such research as the means at his command has permitted, the compiler has found the name in connecnection with no other locality (excepting the neighboring province of Guienne), and therefore considers the assumption reasonable that the American family, though not directly traceable to that section, is of the same nativity as those whose names and deeds have been considered worthy of public record, and are thus preserved to us. To the great regret of the compiler, he has been unable to connect the American family with its French progenitors; indeed, the early history of it prior to the settlement of its head in Norwalk, Connecticut, is unknown, but in the absence of evidence to the contrary, it is safe to consider Alexander Resseguie of Norwalk as the emigrant, and with him properly begins the family history.

It will be of interest, however, to note such facts concerning others of the name as have been found, although largely contemporary with the American family; and beginning in order of date, the first is

Dominique de Resseguier, who, in 1597, resigned his position as secular abbot* of the church of St. Afrodise-de-Beziers.†

---

* Hercule de Gailhac fut nominé par le Roi le 22 Octobre, 1597, à l'abbaye séculiere de Saint Afrodise-de-Beziers sur la démission de Dominique Resseguier. — *Hosiers, Armorial Général.*

† Beziers is a town of Languedoc, in the department of Hérault, dating from 120 B. C.

Jean de Resseguier was born in Toulouse, July 22, 1683, of a family originally of Rouergue,* which for three centuries furnished eminent magistrates to the Parliament of Toulouse.

He, himself, was a member of that body, and president of its Chamber of Inquisition. He was elected judge in 1705, and the same year a member of the Jeux Floraux (a literary institute established in Toulouse in 1322 for the purpose of encouraging the art of poetry); later he became one of the founders of the Academy of Sciences of Toulouse. He died in that city, Sept. 25, 1753, leaving a number of unpublished works, among them a *History of the Parliament of Toulouse*, the manuscript of which is still preserved.

Clement Ignace de Resseguier (knight), son of Jean de Resseguier, was born in Toulouse, Nov. 23, 1724, and was intended from infancy as a member of the order of Malta (an order of chivalry, whose origin is traced to the Crusades); consequently, when young went to the island of Malta, where his vows were performed. After having won distinction in a number of expeditions against the infidels, he became general of the Galleys, amassed wealth, and had the advantage of a long residence in France. Chevalier de Resseguier, though gifted with wit, was naturally caustic, and imprudently directed a number of epigrams against people of influence, which resulted in his imprisonment in the Bastile. A keen satire upon Madame de Pompadour led to his detention in the Castle of If, from which he was released through the intercession of a friend.

The property which he possessed in France having been lost through the Revolution, he retired to Malta, where he was living when the place was surrendered to Bonaparte in 1798. He died the same year and was buried on the island. He was the author of quite a number of published works, both in poetry and prose.

Louis Elizabeth Emanuel de Resseguier, Marquis of Miremont, grandson of Jean, and nephew of Clement Ignace de Resseguier, was born in Toulouse, May 15, 1755, and married Angelique Louise de Chastenet de Puységur, grandniece of the Marshal de Puységur, and niece of the Count de Puységur, minisister of war under Louis XVI. His merit and high reputation gained for him the position of advocate-general, at the age of 24.

---

* Rouergue was an ancient district of France, in the eastern part of the province of Guienne. It is now included in the department of Aveyron.

In 1788 he was called to Versailles to take part in the Second Assembly of the leading notables of the kingdom. The ease with which he dispatched his duties, and the wisdom and sagacity displayed by him, made him a noticeable figure in the Assembly.

Charged by his office of magistrate with the duty of suppressing the popular riots at Toulouse, he was one of the first exposed to the abuses of the Revolution.

At his demand the Parliament of Toulouse refused to transcribe the decrees of the National Assembly, relative to the suppression of the courts of justice throughout the kingdom and the organization of a new judicial order, and he entered before the King and the people a solemn protest against the injuries done to society by the revolutionary innovations. The answer of the National Assembly to this was a decree denouncing the action of the Toulouse Parliament, and stigmatizing the protest of its attorney as the *tocsin of rebellion*, and commanding that the members who had taken a part in it be immediately arrested and brought before a tribunal, to be tried for the crime of rebellion. Fifty-three members of this Parliament died upon the scaffold, but Resseguier was so fortunate as to escape to the Spanish frontier and thence to England.

Returning to France, he concealed himself for a number of years in Paris, until the re-establishment of peace restored him to liberty. He died of a sudden and violent illness, Aug. 28, 1801, as he was about starting to meet his family in Languedoc.

Bernard Marie Jules de Resseguier (Count), son of the preceding, was born in Toulouse, Jan. 28, 1788. His parents having fled from France, he passed several months with his grandmother (wife of the President de Resseguier) in prison, during the Terror, but upon the death of Robespierre regained his liberty. Later he was placed in the military school of Fontainebleau, and in 1806 had completed his studies and immediately entered into service as an officer of cavalry in the campaigns of Spain and Poland. His health having greatly suffered in consequence of the exposure and hardships of a military life, he left the army and returned to his native land, where, in 1811, he married Christine Pauline Charlotte de Mac-Mahon, and continued to reside in Languedoc, devoting himself to poetic composition. His first literary essays opened for him the doors of the Academy of the Jeux Floraux in 1818, and in 1822 he removed to Paris and easily found his place in the foremost ranks of literature. He founded, with others (among them Victor Hugo), in 1823, *The French Muse*, a periodical much in favor in its day, and which took a large share in the contest between the Classical and Romantic schools of literature. Jules de Resseguier inclined toward the Romantic, but without sharing its exaggerations. He was kept from that by two qualities, which he possessed in the highest degree: good taste and good sense. Although imagination was the leading quality of his mind, it had been cultivated in a more serious vein, and his tastes as much as his poetic opinions inclined him to lend his help to the government of the Restoration; he entered the State's Council and was nominated Chevalier of the Legion of Honor at the end of the year 1823, and in his work won high praise and esteem. The essential stimulant to high political career, ambition, was absolutely wanting in Jules de Resseguier, and without ceasing to be faithful to the work of the State's Council, he always kept his preference for a literary life. In 1827 he published a volume of selected pieces under the title of *Poetic Pictures*, and its success was sufficient to definitely mark his literary vocation.

The Revolution of 1830 separated him entirely from politics, and he refused without hesitation the oath of allegiance which the new power asked of him. His leisure was of profit to literature, and secured to the several papers which were founded at that time, a great number of poems and short works of prose fiction, in which the poetic inspiration appeared no less than in the former.

But in the brilliant life of Paris he never forgot his native province, and in 1840 he returned to Toulouse and "Sauveterre," the elegant home which he had built in view of the Pyrenees. The native soil and the domestic hearth became then his habitual themes. His writings, always harmonious and noble, became not more religious, for they had always been so, but more pious in all the sweet acceptations of that word, and also more touching.

His rare qualities were rewarded by a rare domestic happiness, and it was given him to celebrate the fiftieth anniversary of his wedding. He reached the end of his career, strong of mind and of heart. A Christian eloquence which surprised even those who loved and admired him inspired his last days. He met death with serenity and found new accents of tenderness to bless his family gathered around him. He passed away on the 7th of September, 1862, in the 75th year of his age.

He belonged to a family where quickness of wit was hereditary; his sallies were always original and unexpected, but ever within the confines of good breeding.

Those whom he had once attracted never withdrew; as a friend he was always delightful and reliable, and his name will remain the accomplished type of the alliance of the best traditions of the old society with the most brilliant qualities of the new.

Albert de Resseguier (Count), son of the preceding, was born in Toulouse in April, 1816. He completed his studies at the German University, and was the author of a number of published works. He represented the Lower Pyrenees in the Legislative Assembly, and regularly voted with the monarchial and parliamentary majority. He proposed the reduction of the salaries of representatives; the modification of the forest laws; and moved the setting at liberty of Abd-el-Kader. He was a member of the permanent Algerian Commission, and caused to be adopted by the Assembly several propositions relative to this colony. He made a Report upon the regulation of the Laws of Petition, etc., etc.

On the 2d of December, 1851, he was a member of the reunion of the Governors of the Tenth District; signed the decree of the fall of the President of the Republic, and caused his imprisonment at Mont Valerien. He was a member of the municipal council of Pau, and of the general council of the Lower Pyrenees.

NOTE. — The above accounts were chiefly derived from the following works: *Biographie Universelle, Michaud; Dictionnaire des Contemporains, G. Vapereau; Littérature Française Contemporaine;* and *Moniteur des Dates.* Although search has been made through many encyclopedic volumes relating to various topics, and through a number of books of heraldry, nothing further concerning this name has been found.

Whitney, Joseph,	229	Wilford, John Barker, . . 584
" Joyce,	219	Wilkson, Fannie D., . . 448
" Minerva,	220	Williams, Harvey Eliphalet, . 167
" Newberry,	234	Williamson, Sylvia, . . 334
" Phebe,	227	Wilson, Benjamin Rich, . 491
" Polly,	230	" Edward Jonathan, . 492
" Riley,	231	" Sarah Jane, . . 283
" Sarah Ann,	222	Winchell, Ellen Maria, . 411
" Susan,	226	Winne, George, . . 572
" Sunilda,	228	Wood, Ezekiel, Page 20.
" William Lewis,	221	" Solomon, Page 21.
Wilbur, Carr,	82	Worden, Sarah Jane, . . 204
" Elias,	405	
" Jane,	82	Yeoman, ——, Page 24.
" Owen,	403	Young, Amelia C., . . 578
Wilcox, Charles,	331	

THE RESSEGUIE FAMILY.

FIRST GENERATION.

A star (*) prefixed to a name signifies that the person's number and family occur in the succeeding generation, the number being in the center of the line directly over the family record.

I.

Alexander Resseguie was a settler in Norwalk, Conn., in 1709. Tradition has it that he was the younger son of one Alexandre Resseguie, a Huguenot refugee from France, who brought with him from the mother country a small hair-covered trunk, studded with iron nails, containing all of the family wealth he was able to secure, consisting largely of title deeds to property in France. Hoping to some day regain his abandoned possessions, he educated his eldest son to the profession of the law, intending when the time was ripe, he should return to France and establish a claim to the family estates. This hope was destined never to be realized, for the son died just previous to the time of his intended departure on this mission, and the father, disheartened, abandoned the undertaking; the trunk* and papers passed into the possession of the younger son, and at a subsequent period the latter were, the most of them, destroyed by fire.

Just how much of fact underlies this tradition we know not. It is the opinion of the compiler that the family fled to England, before coming to this country, and that one Alexandre de Ressiguier, from Trescléoux, in Dauphiny, who was known as a silk manufacturer in London, in 1696, was the father of Alexander of Norwalk. It is probable that an earlier residence

---

* This trunk is now in the possession of Col. George E. Gray of San Francisco. It is eleven and one-half inches long, seven inches wide, and four inches high; the top oval. The wood is worm-eaten; very little hair remains upon the leather, and the nails with which it is studded are of hammered iron. The papers contained in the trunk were nearly all destroyed by fire, by the wife of Timothy Resseguie (14), during a fit of temporary insanity.

of the family in America would have been a matter of record, but no trace of the name of Resseguie (save one*) has been found prior to the appearance of Alexander in Norwalk, in 1709.

Thus we are compelled to record him as the head of the family, and the ancestor of the American Resseguies. On the first day of April, 1709, he purchased a tract of land of Samuel St. John,† and from this time for many years, he was interested in

---

* "Sigourney and his associates were accompanied on their return to Oxford (in 1697) by a French minister, lately arrived from England. This was Jacques Laborie, a native of Cardaillac, in the province of Guyenne, who had been officiating for several years in certain of the French churches in London. Laborie had ingratiated himself with Lord Bellomont, the new governor, who procured for him a yearly stipend of thirty pounds out of the Corporation money, together with a commission to labor among the Indians near New Oxford. He brought with him his wife *Jeanne de Resseguier*, and his little daughter Susanne. . . . After ministering for some time to the French colony in New Oxford, Mass., and laboring as a missionary among the savages in the vicinity, he went to New York and took charge of the French church in that city, as Peiret's successor, for two years, Oct. 15, 1704, to Aug. 25, 1706. After this he engaged in the practice of medicine and surgery, and as early as the year 1716 settled in Fairfield County, Conn., as a physician, occasionally assisting the Church of England missionary."—*The Huguenot Emigration to America, by C. W. Baird.* It is possible that Jeanne de Resseguier was a relative of Alexander, perhaps a sister, and that her emigration to this country was the bond that drew him hither. The residence of both in Fairfield County, if not accountable for in this way, was a rather singular coincidence.

†*Copy of deed.* "To all people to whom these presents shall come, Greeting. Know ye that I, Samuel St. John of ye town of Norwalk in ye county of Fairfield, within his majesties Colony of Connecticut, in New England. For and in consideration of ye sum of six pounds current provision pay of said Colony to me in hand before the Ensealing hereof well and truly paid by Alexander Resseguie of ye aforesaid Town and County, the Receipt whereof I do hereby acknowledge and myself therewith fully satisfied and contented, Have given, granted, bargained, sold, and by these presents do trooly, fully and absolutely give, grant, bargain, sell, aliene, convey and confirm unto him ye said Alexander Resseguie, his heirs and assigns forever, a certain piece of Land lying within the Township of Norwalk aforesaid, near unto and bearing South West from ye Land called ye Heth. Containing by Estimation, Five Acres and three Roods, be it more or less. Bounded in ye Southwest by ye Land of David Tuttle, North West by ye said St. Johns Land, North East and South East by Common Land. To Have and to Hold, said granted and bargained premises with all the appurtenances, priviledges and comodities to ye same belonging or in anywise appertaining to him the Said Alexander Resseguie, his heirs and assigns forever. To his and their only proper use, comfitt and behoof forever, And that the said Alexander Resseguie, his heirs and assigns shall and may from time to time and at all times forever hereafter by

acquiring land, the records showing one hundred or more estates to which he held the titles, located in what is now comprised in the towns of Norwalk, Wilton, Ridgefield, New Canaan, Westport, and Weston. The ability to make these large acquisitions would seem to indicate the substantial character of the contents of the hair trunk.

On the 19th day of October, 1709, Alexander Resseguie married Sara Bontecou, daughter of Pierre* and Marguerite (Collinot) Bontecou of New York. She was born in France and reached New York with her parents in 1689. The summer preceding his marriage was probably spent in preparing a home, which, though its exact location cannot be pointed out, was undoubtedly in the extreme southern part of Ridgefield, a new town created from lands purchased of the Indians the year previous.† We have evidence that he soon began the career of a

---

force and virtue of these presents Lawfully, peaceably and quietly have, hold, use, occupie, possess and injoy Said Demised and bargained premises with ye appurtenances free and clear, And freely and clearly acquitted, Exonerated and Discharged of, from all and all manner of former and other gifts, grants, bargains, Sales, Leases, Mortgages and other Incumbrances Whatsoever. Furthermore, I the said Samuell Saint John, for myself my heirs Executor and administrators Do Covenant and Ingage ye above Demised premises to him the said Alexander Resseguie, his heirs and assigns against the Lawfull claims or Demands of any person or persons whatsoever forever hereafter to Warrant Secure and Defend. In witness whereof I have here unto sett my hand and Seale this first day of Aprill in ye year of our Lord one thousand seven hundred and nine, and in ye Eighth year of her majesties Reign, Queen Ann.

Signed, Sealed and Delivered in ye presence of us witnesses.

THO. HANFORD,   SAMUEL SAINT JOHN.

JOSEPH SAINT JOHN.

Samuel Saint John, the Grantor and Subscriber to ye above Written Instrument, personally Appeared on ye first Day of Aprill, 1709, and Did acknowledg ye same to be his free and Voluntary Act and Deed.

Before me,   JAMES OLMSTEED,
Justice of peace.

Recorded Aprill 6th, 1709.
Per JOHN COPP, *Record'r.*

*The compiler of this work is a descendant of Pierre Bontecou, through the line of his son Timothy. It was the original intention to publish a genealogical history of all his descendants, but so far as the Resseguie line is concerned this object has been defeated, as explained in the introduction.

†"In 1708, John Belden, Samuel Keeler, Matthew Seymour, Matthias St. John, and other inhabitants of Norwalk, to the number of twenty-five, pur-

farmer, and had, in a short time, wrested part of his land from the grasp of the forest and reduced it to a condition of tillage, by the following extract from the Colonial Records:

"Newhaven, August 9th. 1711. The Colony of Connecticut is debtor to sundry persons in money, as followeth, that is to say . . . To Mr. Alexander Russigue of Norwalk, for 40 bushels wheat taken out of Mr. Jno Williams' sloop at New Haven, at 4s. 6d. per bushel. 9. o. o."

Until his death he evidently pursued the even tenor of his way as a private citizen and pioneer farmer, holding no office, and probably wanting none, and leaving but little trace of his life save the record of his possessions. He died in October, 1752. His wife survived him until May, 1757. The place of their sepulchre is unknown, but it was probably in the old cemetery in the southern part of Ridgefield, in which but two ancient stones remain to mark the spot where many lie interred. The following is the will of Alexander Resseguie:

"In the name of God, Amen. I, Alexander Resseguie, formerly of Ridgefield, now of Norwalk in ye County of Fairfield and Colony of Connecticut, being weak of body but of a disposing mind and memory, praised be God; calling to mind ye mortality of my body, and yt is appointed for all men once to die, do make and ordain this my last will and testament. That is to say principally and first of all I give and bequeath my soul to God who gave it; and my body I recommend to be decently buryed at ye discretion of my execrs hereafter named, nothing doubting but at ye generall ressurrection I shall receive ye same again by ye mighty power of God to bless me within this life. I give, demise and dispose of ye same as followeth, my just debts and funerall charges being first paid:

I give and bequeath to well beloved wife Sarah, ye use & improvement of ye one-half part of my house & barn and homlot, said building standing or lying in ye southerly part of Ridgefield Town, during ye terme or time she shall remain my widow.

ITEM. I give and bequeath unto my loving sons Alexander, Abraham, Isaac and Jacob, all my land and reall estate that I shall die possessed of or have any right to; except what I have before given away by deed of gift to them and their heirs and assigns forever, to be equally divided amongst them my said four sons.

Lastly, I do hereby appoint, constitute and fully impower my well beloved wife Sarah to be my executrix, together with my loving son Alexander Resse-

---

chased a large tract between that town and Danbury. The purchase was made of Catoonah, the chief sachem, and other Indians, who were the proprietors of that part of the country. The deed bears date Sept. 30, 1708. At this session (1709) it was ordained that it should be a distinct township, by the name of Ridgefield."— *History of Connecticut*, by Benj. Trumbull, D.D., Vol. I., page 460.

guie executor of this my last will and testament; and do hereby disannul & revoke all former wills and testaments by me made, ratifying and confirming this & no other to be my last will and testament.

In witness whereof I have hereunto set my hand & seal this 3¹ day of October Anno Dom. 1752.

ALEXANDER RESSEGUIE.

Signed, sealed, published, pronounced & declared by ye said Alexander Resseguie, ye testator, to be his last will & testament. I presence of us, ye subscribers.

SAML OLMSTED,
EZRA HICCOK,
THAD. MEAD.

NORWALK, October ye 24th ins., A. D. 1752.

Then personally appeared Saml Olmsted, Ezra Hickock, and Thadeus Mead, ye evidences to within written will and gave oath yt they see Mr. Alexander Resseguie, now dec'd, sign, seal, and heard him declare ye same to be his last will and testament, and yt they judged him to be sound in mind and judgment at ye same time and yt they signed as evidences at ye same time in presents of ye testator. Before me,

SAMLL SMITH,
Justice of peace.

Att a court of Probate held in Fairfield Decenr 19th, 1752, Personally appeared Sarah Resseguie named executrix & Alexander Resseguie named executor to ye foregoing will & exhibited said will to said court in order for probation and they then accepted ye trust committed to them by ye testator. said will being proved is by said court approved and ordered to be recorded.

Test. DAVID BURR, *Clerk.*"

"AUG. ye 14th, 1754.

An Inventory of Mr Alexander Resseguies Estate late of Ridgefield, dec'd &c.

We the subscribers being appointed and sworn as ye law directs to take the Inventory of the Estate of the above sd Resseguie Dec'd, and have done it in ye manner following, viz:

		£	s.	d.
1	feather bead @.	15	0	0
1	do	3	0	0
2	Dutch Blankets.	3	10	0
1	Rugg @ £12.			
1	Diamond Coverlet £5.	17	0	0
	Ye Green Curtains, Vallents & head cloth.	4	0	0
3	Pillows & Pillo beirs	4	0	0
1	Bolster. £2. ye Sirue Bedstead £5.	7	0	0
1	Feather Bed.	10	0	0
1	Bed Ticken.	2	0	0
a	Bedquilt.	6	0	0
3	Blankets	7	15	0
1	Bolster. & 2 Pillows and pillow beers.	3	10	0

		£	s.	d.
1 Bedstead & cord.		3	0	0
5 Pr Cotton sheets.		25	0	0
7 sheets.		12	0	0
1 Bed & Furniture.		12	0	0
2 fine Table cloths.		5	0	0
3 do of Huckerbark		9	0	0
1 do		1	6	0
9 fine napkins.		13	10	0
10 do		3	0	0
4 do		1	4	0
a Desk		12	0	0
a Small chest of Drawers.		3	0	0
1 Trunk £5. to a Small do. £2.		7	0	0
a Table £5. to a Round Table. 40.s. 1 do. 10s.		7	10	0
a Case with 4 Bottles.		1	12	0
a Large Looking Glass.		16	0	0
a Great Chair.		1	12	0
6 Black chairs.		6	0	0
5 other chairs.		4	6	0
a Great wheel.		1	0	0
1 Old Trunk. 12.s. 1 Small do 12.s.		1	4	0
a Cupboard with feet. 8.s. 1. Hanging Do. 34.s.		2	2	0
11 Knives & 12 Forks. 48.s. a pair of Scales 5.s. & a pr of money Scales. 20s. Old Ink Pot. 4s.		3	17	0
a large Brass Kittle.		20	0	0
1 Do. £9. to 1 Do £8. one Do 25.s.		18	5	0
1 Iron Kettle.		1	10	0
4 Silver Spoons.		24	0	0
3 Smaller Silver Spoons		3	10	0
a Small Silver cup.		3	8	0
1 Stone Platter.			10	0
4 Earthern Platters.		2	5	0
5 Earthern Platters 40.s. to 2. Small do. 8.s.		2	8	0
a Speckled Earthern Pot. 10s. one with a Lid. 8.s.			18	0
1 Small Do. 3.s.			3	0
3 Small Earthern Plates.			6	0
1 Punch Bowl.			8	0
5 Earthern Tea Cups & Plates			15	0
6 China Tea Cups & 4 Plates.		1	12	0
a Large Pr of Steelyards		7	0	0
a Small Do.		1	5	0
an old Iron Pot.		1	0	0
an Iron Chain.		3	10	0
a narrow ax 40.s. an old Hatchet. 4.s.		2	4	0
a Service Book.		2	0	0
a Water Pail.			5	0
a Brass Lid			10	0

	£	s.	d.
a Pr of And-Irons	10	0	0
2 Pr of Curtain Rods of Iron.	1	10	0
a close stool	5	0	0
an Iron Bed Candlestick.	3	0	0
a Brass Candlestick.	1	0	0
a Hanging Do.	1	0	0
a Candlestick.		8	0
a peal & Tongs.		16	0
Grid-Iron 50.s. a Small Do. 20.s.	3	10	0
2 Chafing Dishes	2	0	0
a Toasting Iron. 16.s. a Flesh Fork. 6.s.	1	2	0
2 Pepper Boxes. 8.s. one Brass Scimmer @ 16.s.	1	4	0
a Pr of Brass Scales with Lead weights	2	0	0
42 lb. of Good Pewter.	37	16	0
14½ lb. of Pewter.	8	11	0
5 lb. of old Pewter.	2	10	0
a tin Callender,		12	0
1 Hoe.		5	0
42½ lb of old Iron.	4	3	0
a Small Mortar & Pestle. 60.s. a pepper mill 12.s.			
2 canisters.	4	4	0
a Coffee Pott & 2 Sugar Boxes, 2 Gimblets	1	0	0
a Water Pott	1	0	0
a round Coulered a Tea Table.	2	0	0
31 lb. & ¾ of Leather.	14	5	9
a Copper Pye Pan.	6	0	0
a Brass Skillett 40.s. 1 do. 16.s.	2	16	0
a Cedar Tubb,		16	0
a Pr of old Tongs & Old Iron.		13	6
a 2 Handle'd Stone Pott.		16	0
a Tea Kettle.	5	10	0
an Iron Spitt 20.s. 1 Do. 17.s.	1	17	0
an Iron Pott 45s. 1 Do. 20.s.	3	5	0
an Iron Goose.		10	0
an Iron Tramel. 58.s. 1. Do 30.s.	4	8	0
Ye French Books.	1	0	0
a Negro Wench & child.	350	0	0
a large mare.	90	0	0
a Colt, comeing a year old.	40	0	0
Money of New York Currency @ 8.s. pr oz.	15	5	0
Connecticut Money of New Tenor as it stands in ye full of ye Bill,	27	0	0
a note of New York Currency, @ 8s. per oz.	37	0	0
1 Do of	50	0	0
1 Do of	70	0	0
1 Do of	70	0	0
1 Do of	18	0	0

	£	s.	d.
1 note of Connecticut money, old tenor	100	0	0
1 note of Old Tenor.	10	0	0
1 Do. of Old Tenor.	15	0	0
1 Do	14	0	0
1 Do	13	0	0
Ye Book of Debts.	288	1	2
Land in Norwalk near Alexander Resseguies House at ye Salt Branch about 19 acres & ¼ at	312	0	0
8 acres of meadow Land, the meadow Land above Bethel Heacock's.	500	0	0
12 acres of Bogg meadow by ye above sd Land.	96	0	0
About fifty-four acres & three Roods. by ye above said Land.	1,314	0	0
6 acres near Ridgefield Line above Seymour's Barn.	60	0	0
a fifty Pounds Wright in ye Comons.	4	0	0
a Part in a Place where 'twill do to set a mill.	2	0	0
1 Acre near Capt. Danll Sainjohn's House In Ridgefield, ...	50	0	0
The House & Barn & three acres of Land & ye norwest Part of the Land that lies Easterly from Jonah Keelers Homestead with ye orchard and all ye Privileges standing upon sd 3 acres of Land at	1,150	0	0
And to ye Rest of ye Land yt lies adjoining to ye above sd Land at	1,750	0	0
Ye Land at ye high Ridge so called at	375	0	0
Ye Land yt is called Abrahams Homelot at	240	0	0
2 acres of Land yt lies below ye Lane called Resseguies Lane .	50	0	0
About 20 acres of Land at ye upper End of Millers Ridge so called, with ye Buildings on part of ye same, ...	700	0	0
Ye three half lots in ye Great Swamp, ...	182	10	0
12 acres of Land at ye Lower End of ye Millers Ridge below Matthew Benedicts Land.	400	0	0
Five acres at ye old Spectacle Lott.	140	0	0
8 acres of upland at ye Brimstone Lott.	128	0	0
Eight acres of upland at ye Lot below whipstick Ridge. so called.	192	0	0
17 acres at Brimstone Swamp.	229	10	0
3 acres of ye Little Swamp.	36	0	0
About 53 acres & ¼ of ye Bluff Land.	428	0	0
a half Lot of ye 5th 20 acre Division.	45	0	0
a half lot of ye 6th 20 acre Division.	30	0	0
a half lot of ye 7th 20 acre division.	30	0	0
Half a right in ye Commons.	40	0	0
an old Knot Bowl. 3 s. & an Earthen Pitcher. 5 s. . . .		8	0
A Sett of Callicoe Curtains & Vallants.	12	0	0
8 pillow beers & 7 small Do. all	12	0	0

	£	s.	d.
a small Iron pot 4.s. a Hammer 4 s.		8	0
a Dutch wheel 40.s. a Real 12.s. a pr of sheep shears 8.s.	3	0	0
a Cotton Coverlet £6. & an old Carpet for a Bed 30.s.	7	10	0
a 2 qt Pewter 40.s. a qt Do. 30.s. & a pt Do.	4	10	0
large 2 handle Knot Bowl 40.s. & a rown Do. 24.s.	3	4	0
Milk Tray & to a smaller Do.		10	0
a post ax & a stubbing Hoe. & a garden Hoe. & old froe.	1	0	0
a Box Iron & heaters & a cold Iron	2	0	0
a Knot Bowl at 18.s.		18	0
an old chain & Pitchford.	1	10	0
150 feet of whitewood Board.	3	0	0
100 foot of whitewood Boards more	2	0	0
2 pr spectacles & cases.		10	0
	£10,514	12	5

A true copy of ye original.
Recorded pr D. BURR. *Clerk.*

BENJA HOYT
MATTHEW BENEDICT } *Appraisers.*
EZRA HICKOK.

RIDGEFIELD, Augt ye 14th 1754.

To Coll And' Burr. Jude of Probate. for ye District of Fairfield. — Sir these are to enform you that ye widow Sarah Resseguie & Relict and ye heirs of ye late dec'd Alexander Resseguie, declared before us the subscribers that ye Cloathing & Saddle of ye sd Dec'd were divided to ye four Heirs of the sd dec'd to their acceptance before ye above sd Inventory was taken, as witness our Hands ye date above sd.

EZRA HICKOK
BENJA HOYT
MATTHEW BENEDICT

At a Court of Probate held in Fairfield. Aug't 16. A. D. 1754. Personally appeared Alexander Resseguie, one of ye Exec'* of ye Last Will & Testament of Alexander Resseguie, late of Ridgefield dec'd, & Exhibited ye foregoing Inventory to sd Court & made oath yt ye same is a true & perfect Inventory of all ye Estate of sd Dec'd yt he knows of, and if anything further shall appear belonging to sd Estate he will cause it to be added: sd Inventory being proved, is by sd Court approved. & ordered to be recorded.

Test. DAVID BURR, *Clerk.*"

It would be interesting to note the distribution of this large estate to the heirs, but no record of such distribution can be found. After the death of the mother, her personal estate, con- consisting chiefly of wearing apparel and household belongings, amounting in value to £182 6s. 6½d., was divided among the four sons.*

CHILDREN. (*Second Generation.*)

*2.	I.	ALEXANDER, b. Aug. 27, 1710.
3.	II.	PETER, b. Dec. 19, 1711; probably d. young.
*4.	III.	JAMES, b. Nov. 6, 1713.
*5.	IV.	ABRAHAM, b. July 27, 1715.
*6.	V.	ISAAC, b. May 24, 1717.
*7.	VI	JACOB, b. Aug. 14, 1719.
8.	VII.	SARAH, b. July 12, 1721; d. May 25, 1753.

* "At a Court of Probate held in Fairfield, Feby 15th 1758. Alexr Resseguie Admr on ye Estate of Sarah Russegui late of Norwalk decd, having made application to this Court and prayed yt ye time assigned him for rendering an Acct of his Adminsº on sd Estate may be lengthened out & having offered sufficient reason therefor, this Court allows to sd Administr further Time (viz) untill ye first Tuesday in June next."

"At a Court of Probate held in Fairfield, June 15. A. D. 1758, Whereas, an Inventory of the Estate of Sarah Resseguie late decd hath been exhibited, amounting with ye Credits to the sum of £290.. 19s.. 0¼¹, Lawful money, and an amount of Debts hath been rendred amounting to £107.. 12s.. 6d.. like money, which being deducted from sd Inventory, and Credits, leaves the sum of £182.. 6s. 6½ , Lawfull money, Clear Estate, which this Court orders to be divided to and among the Children of sd decd in the following manner, viz:

To Alexander Resseguie being ye Eldest Son, Two shares, or a double Portion, and to Abraham, Isaac & Jacob Ressiguie, Each a Single Share — and this Court doth appoint and Impower Messrs Samll Olmstead of Ridgfield and David Lambert and Ezra Heacock of Norwalk, being Freeholders and disinterested to make Division thereof accordingly.

Test.   DAVID ROWLAND, *Clerk.*

SECOND GENERATION.

2.

Alexander Resseguie, Jr., born Aug. 27, 1710; married in Wilton, Conn., Feb. 16, 1737-8. Thankful Belden. Their dates of death are unknown, but both were living in 1793. But little has been learned concerning Alexander, Jr. He was one of the heirs named in his father's will, and received from his mother's estate a "double portion," as the eldest son, one-half of it consisting of a "negro wench," whose value was set down at forty pounds. He was the possessor of much real estate, largely inherited from his father, and like him appears to have devoted his time to agriculture and the improvement of his lands. Silver ore, which, to some extent, has been found in that section of Connecticut, existed upon his property, and in 1675 a mine was opened, located near the northern boundary of the town of Wilton, and a lease* of the property for one hundred years granted

---

* "This Indenture made the seventeenth day of May 1765, between Alexander Resseguie of Norwalk, in the County of Fairfield and Colony of Connecticut, of the one part, and Samuel Betts, Nathan Hubbell, Matthew Mead, Matthew Mervine, James Olmsted, Jun', Silas Olmsted, Joseph Rockwell, Jun', Jesse Ogden, all of Norwalk, and Matthew Fountain of Bedford in West Chester County, and province of New York, of the other part, witnesseth, that the s^d Alexander Resseguie as well in Consideration of the Cost and Charges which the said Samuell Betts (et al) must necessarily expend in and about the undertaking, adventures and works hereafter mentioned, and in Consideration of Reservation & Covenants hereafter mentioned Contained by and on the parts of the said Samuel Betts. (et al) their heirs, Executors and Administrators and Assigns, free Liberty, License and Authority, from time to time and at all or any time or times During the Term hereafter mentioned, to Dig, Search, work for, and raise all such Lead ore, or Copper ore, Tin ore, and all other ores and minerals whatsoever, which can or shall or may be found, Digged, gotten up or raised, as well in, from, or out of all or any part or parts of the Lands or grounds of or belonging to the said Alexander Resseguie, situate and lying in the Township of sd Norwalk near the Dwelling House of Azor Belden, in quantity about forty acres, bounded north by John Belden, Easterly, Ezekiel Wood, South by Ezekiel Wood, and Solomon

to certain parties for the purpose of taking out the ore. In 1774 Alexander deeded this property to his son William, subject to the above named lease. During the Revolutionary war the mine was filled with brush and rubbish, undoubtedly for the purpose of keeping its existence secret from the British, who at times abounded in that region. It remained in this condition until 1876, when it was cleaned out and a company formed for the purpose of working it, but a question arising as to the validity of title, and the prospect of success being considered too vague

---

Wood's heirs, West by highway, . . . and liberty of ingress, Egress to and for the said Samuel Betts (et al) their heirs, Executors, Administrators & assigns, and their servants and workmen at all times during the term hereafter mentioned, with horses and carriages to and from the same, except and always Reserved out of the said grant, unto the said Alexander Resseguie, his heirs and assigns, one full equal eight part, the whole into eight equal parts being divided, of and in the said ores and minerals which shall arise, be digged and gotten in the lands aforesaid, after the same is pounded and washed and fitted for Refining, free of all charges of the same, for and in Lease of the Toll and farm, to be had and taken by the said Alexander Resseguie, his heirs and assigns in such manner as is hereafter mentioned. To have and to hold all and singular, sd Libertys and privileges before Leased, unto the sd Samuel Betts (*et al.*) their heirs, executors, administrators, and from the day of the date hereof for and during the term of one hundred years next ensuing, fully to be completed and ended, yielding and delivering unto the said Resseguie, his heirs and assigns the said one eighth part, the whole into eight equal parts being divided, hereinbefore excepted, of all of the ores and minerals which shall be so digged, raised, after the same is pounded and fitted for refining, out of the lands aforesaid or any part thereof as aforesaid, and to have, hold and enjoy their remaining seven eights parts thereof, to them, their heirs, Executors, Administrators & assigns to their own proper use and uses as aforesaid. As witness whereof we have set our hands and seals. The consideration of the above written instrument is such that if the above mentioned persons shall continue to carry on and prosecute the above mentioned enterprise, then this Lease to stand in full force, otherwise to be null and void.

James Olmsted. Jr.	Alexander Resseguie
Silas Olmsted.	Sam¹ Betts.
Joseph Rockwell Jr.	Nathan Hubbell
Jesse Ogden.	Matthew Mead
Matthew Fountain,	Matt. Mervine."

Signed Sealed & Delivered
 In presence of
Thadd Hubbell.
Ephm Kimberly.
Peter Hubbell.   (Norwalk Town Records.)

to warrant the necessary expenditure, it was soon abandoned by its projectors.

Undoubtedly the large property formerly held by the senior Alexander, and bequeathed by him to his children, became largely reduced by the events connected with the Revolutionary war, which depreciated property everywhere and proved the financial ruin of so many people. The family became scattered and the closing years of the eighteenth century found them located widely apart. No stone marks the burial place of Alexander and his wife, but probably the old cemetery in Ridgefield received their remains. The will of Alexander Resseguie is dated July 27, 1793. It was written in a beautiful script upon two pages of a sheet, the lower half of which has been burned away. It is a relic of the hair trunk noted on page 10. The legible portion of the will is here given. No record of its probate has been found.

"In the name of Almighty God; Amen:— this 27th day of July A. D. 1793: — I Alexander Resseguie of Ridgefield, in the District of Danbury, being advanced in Age, but thro' the goodness of God of a Sound mind and Memory; being desirous to set my house in Order, Do for that purpose make and Ordain this my last Will & Testament;— that is to say;— First of all I give and Recommend my Immortal Spirit into the hands of God who gave it, hoping for Acceptance with him, and the Eternal Life in the World to come, through the Merits of Jesus Christ, my Lord and Savior;— & my Body to the Dust from whence it was taken, (believing in the Resurrection from the Dead) to be Buried in a Decent Christian like manner;— (after my Decease) at the Discretion of my Executors herein named;— & as to what Worldly Goods and Estates it hath pleased God to Bless me with; I hereby Give, Bequeath, and Dispose thereof in the following form and manner. . . . (Bottom of page missing.)

ITEM,— I hereby declare that what I have already given to my son William to be his full part, and portion of my Estate.

ITEM,— I hereby Give & Bequeath unto my sons Timothy, and Daniel, & to their Heirs and Assigns, the whole of my Real Estate to be equally Divided (after my own and Wife's Decease), between them and their respective Heirs.

LASTLY,— I hereby Constitute, Appoint, Ordain and fully Impower my Well beloved & faithfull Son Timothy, and my well beloved Wife, Thankfull, to be the Executors of this my last Will & Testament, and I hereby order them to cause the same to be fulfilled in every part and particular thereof; & I hereby revoke and Disannul all former Wills & Testaments by me made; hereby declaring this, & this only, to be my last Will & Testament; . . .

Signed, Sealed, Pronounced, and declared, by the Testator to be his last Will and Testament; In the presence of" (Bottom of page missing.)

SECOND GENERATION.

CHILDREN. (*Third Generation.*)

9.	I.	SARAH, b. Nov. 26, 1738; d. July 5, 1745.
*10.	II.	MARGARET, b. Feb. 20, 1741; m. Joseph Riggs.
11.	III.	ALEXANDER, b. Sept. 9, 1743; d. July 16, 1745.
*12.	IV.	ALEXANDER, b. Dec. 10, 1745.
*13.	V.	WILLIAM, b. ——.
*14.	VI.	TIMOTHY, b. Dec. 28, 1754.
*15.	VII.	DANIEL, b. May 1, 1760.
*16.	VIII.	MARY, b. 1764; m. Thomas Cole.

4.

James Resseguie, born Nov. 6, 1713. A thorough search of records and diligent inquiry, fails to gain much information concerning him. The only scrap attainable besides the record of his birth, relates to the fact that he died in the French and Indian War. That he married and had a family is beyond question, for circumstantial evidence points to him as the progenitor of a goodly line of descendants. In the absence of documentary evidence this may be considered amply sufficient to justify the place given him by the compiler.

CHILDREN. (*Third Generation.*)

*17.	I.	JAMES, b. 1744.
*18.	II.	SARAH, b. ——; m. Seth Bouton.
*19.	III.	ABRAHAM, b. ——.

5.

Abraham Resseguie, born July 27, 1715; married Jane ——————, who died July 31, 1797, aged 81. He was one of the heirs to his father's estate. His death occurred previously to that of his wife.

CHILDREN. (*Third Generation.*)

*20.	I.	ABIGAIL, b. ——; m. Jesse Nichols.
*21.	II.	JANE, b. 1750; m. Nathan Smith.
*22.	III.	RACHEL, b. April 11, 1752; m. John Peck.
*23.	IV.	PHEBE, b. March 31, 1754; m. Asa Prime.
*24.	V.	HANNAH, b May 9, 1757; m. Samuel Nichols.
*25.	VI.	JOHN, b. April 2, 1758.

6.

Isaac Resseguie, born May 24, 1717. We know but little about him. He lived first at Ridgefield, and was one of the heirs under his father's will, and received also his portion of his mother's estate. He removed over the border into New York, and evidently settled upon land owned by Colonel Roger Morris, holding as a tenant, for June 4, 1782, he purchased of the commissioners of forfeiture,* for the sum of £58 10s. this land, which is described as follows:

"Situate in Fredericksburgh Precinct,† Dutchess county, in possession of Isaac Russegue. Beginning at a stake and stones by the road in the line of Duke Foster's land, then in the line of said Foster's land north seventy degrees west, thirteen chains, eighty links, to a stake twenty-five links west from a white oak sapling marked: then in the line of Isaac Perce's land, south fifteen degrees west fifty chains seventy-five links, to a black oak stump with stones on it in the line of John Ganung's land: thence in the line of said Ganung's land south forty-two degrees east twenty-nine chains to a stake at said Ganung's northeast corner in the line of Yeoman's land on the westerly bank of Croton River, then north eighteen degrees east thirty chains, eighty links, to a large black oak tree marked, at the southwest corner of said Foster's land, then north three degrees west thirty-three chains seventy-five links to the beginning, containing one hundred and thirty acres more or less."

We do not know that Isaac Resseguie married, unless the following extract from the Redding (Conn.) Church records, refers to him: "Dec. 28, 1766, Simon, son of Isaaih (Isaack?) and Sarah Russica." (Baptized.) If this is intended for our Isaac, and he had a son Simon, no further evidence has been found of his existence.

---

* "A strip 580 rods wide along the east border of the county constitutes a part of the 'oblong tract' and was patented by Thomas Hawley and his associates June 8, 1731. The remaining part of the county (Putnam) and a small part of Dutchess, are included in the great Highland Patent of Adolph Philipse. At the time of the Revolution this Patent was owned by Philip Philipse, and Mary and Susannah, wives of Colonel Roger Morris and Beverly Robinson, of the British army. Morris and Robinson, together with their wives, were attainted, and their property was confiscated and sold by the Commissioners of Forfeiture, chiefly to their former tenants." — *French's Gazetteer of New York*, page 540-1.

† Frederickstown Precinct was formed March 24, 1772, and was named for Frederick Philipse. It included the present towns of Carmel and Kent. Kent was formed as Frederickstown March 7, 1788: its name was changed to Frederick, March 17, 1795, and to Kent, April 15, 1817. The town received its present name from the Kent family who were early settlers. Carmel and a part of Patterson were taken off in 1795.

7.

Jacob Resseguie, born Aug. 14, 1719; married Mary Curtis of Stratford, Conn. (perhaps the daughter of Nathan and Eunice (Judson) Curtis). She died March 17, 1797. aged 77 years. He died Dec. 27, 1801. They lived in Ridgefield. By his will, made March 13, 1799. and probated Jan. 28, 1802. he bequeathed to his daughter, Mary Burt, five shillings; to his daughter Hannah, £60; the remainder to be divided equally between his two sons, Jacob and Alexander. His estate inventoried at $2,233.27.

CHILDREN. (*Third Generation.*)

*26. I. MARY, b. April 7, 1747; m. David Burt.
*27. II. JACOB, b. June 5, 1752.
28. III. ABIJAH, b. Dec. 13, 1754; died unmarried.
*29. IV. ALEXANDER, b. May 24, 1759.
30. V. HANNAH, b. ——; d. in Southeast, N. Y., Jan. 24, 1811. By her father's will she received £60.

THIRD GENERATION.

10.

Margaret Resseguie, born Feb. 20, 1741; died in Ballston, N. Y., Oct. 10, 1842. She married, Sept. 18, 1764, Joseph Riggs,* as his second wife. He was born in Stamford, Conn., May 18, 1738, and died June 15, 1805. In seeking information relative to Mrs. Riggs, the compiler received from her great-grandson the following, given under the caption " Recollections of my Great-Grandmother Riggs when about One Hundred Years of Age," which will be of undoubted interest to the reader.

"She was of a little more than medium height and as straight as any of the girls and boys in their teens. She had a vivid recollection of the scenes and incidents of the Revolutionary War, and of the important events that led to the war, as well as those that succeeded. She was remarkably vivacious, enjoyed society; indeed, was highly social and was 'good company,' as we say. Her sight was somewhat dim, but not so much so that she could not see to go about the house, and even out the door. Her hearing was poor in one ear, while with the other she could hear quite well. . . . In the autumn after grandfather's death, my father and grandmother Riggs started for Groton (Tompkins County, N. Y.), to go with her to Ballston. They went by private conveyance to Syracuse, and reached that place, distant about forty miles, near the middle of the afternoon, and did not get their dinner until then. They were all tired and hungry, but great-grandmother, as she pushed back from the table after a hearty meal, remarked, 'I am quite refreshed, as the boy said when he got a whipping.' She, although in her one hundred and first year, endured the journey quite as well as any of the party. I think I have been told that when she was about sixty years of age she had a severe sickness, and was bed-ridden for many years (I think fifteen), when she got up. One day, when left alone, she worked her feet off the bed and finally managed

---

* Joseph Riggs was the son of Miles and Elizabeth (Whitney) Riggs, and first married Aug. 4, 1761, at New Canaan, Conn., his cousin, Mary Keeler, who was baptized at New Canaan, May 16, 1742, and was the daughter of Daniel and Hannah (Whitney) Keeler. They had one child, Jonathan, who married Jan. 1, 1792, at Norwalk, Conn., Esther Keeler, and whose children were: 1. Julia, born Jan. 5, 1793. 2. James, born April 13, 1794; died Oct. 2, 1795. 3. John Woodward, born Jan. 29, 1796. 4. Esther, born Feb. 4, 1798.

to sit up, got hold of a chair and by its aid managed to take a step or two, but did not go far before she fell, but she continued her efforts and succeeded in learning to walk, a second time, after she was seventy-five years old."

CHILDREN. (*Fourth Generation.*)

*31. I. JAMES, b. June 29, 1765.
*32. II. MILES, b. Sept. 10, 1767.
33. III. IRA, b. Nov. 24, 1769; d. Dec. 23, 1771.
*34. IV. TIMOTHY, b. Oct. 29, 1772.
*35. V. SARAH, b. May 6, 1778; m. Raymond Taylor.
36. VI. ESTHER, b. June 18, 1784; d. in West Troy, N. Y., May, 1862. She married Jedediah Beckwith, as his second wife. She had no children.

12.

Alexander Resseguie, born Dec. 10, 1745; died May 5, 1777. He married in Weston, Conn., July 26, 1771, Eunice Blackman. They lived in Connecticut, probably in Wilton or Ridgefield. Their marriage is found in the Weston church records.

CHILDREN. (*Fourth Generation.*)

37. I. ESTHER, b. Nov. 23, 1771. She m. a Mr. Lobdell, and had a daughter Abigail. It is thought she lived in Greenbush, N. Y.
38. II. THANKFUL, b. Sept. 18, 1773; d. Jan. 19, 1775.
*39. III. ALEXANDER, b. April 18, 1777.

13.

William Resseguie.* The dates of his birth and death have not been learned. He married, in Weston, Conn., Dec. 16, 1771, Susannah Patrick. The homestead in Ridgefield was deeded to him by his father, and is the property referred to in the will of Alexander, Jr. Subsequently he removed to Fishkill, N. Y., where he purchased about 400 acres of land. His son Stephen is said to have had a full family record, which was burned with his house and is much to be regretted, as we are left with very meager data relative to the early record.

---

* The compiler has experienced greater difficulty in obtaining data relative to William Resseguie and his descendants, and with less satisfactory results, than in all other lines combined, and the apparent uselessness of further waiting has decided him to close the work in a somewhat imperfect state; but notwithstanding its imperfection, he is disposed to congratulate himself that the labor bestowed upon it has resulted more favorably than at one time seemed possible.

CHILDREN.* (*Fourth Generation.*)

*40.   I.   WILLIAM, b. ———.
*41.   II. STEPHEN, b. 1774.
*42.   III. NOAH, b. ———.
*43.   IV. SAMUEL, b. March 12, 1776.
*44.   V.   SARAH, b. ———; m. William Botsford.
*45.   VI. SUSAN, b. April 18, 1796; m. Jeremiah Whitney.
*46.   VII. THANKFUL, b. ———; m. Ebenezer Robinson.

14.

Timothy Resseguie, born in Ridgefield, Conn., Dec. 28, 1754; died in Verona, Oneida County, N. Y., Jan. 19, 1838. He married, June 5, 1785, Abigail Lee, daughter of John Lee. She was born Oct. 27, 1760, and died in Verona, May 11, 1834.

Timothy Resseguie served in the Revolutionary War, and married after his return from the service. He remained in Ridgefield three years, assisting his father in the promotion of his farming operations, but at the end of that period concluded to make a home for his family in New York State. As an inducement to his remaining upon the paternal acres his father deeded to him the homestead, but he declined the gift, and, shouldering his knapsack, footed it through the country to Ballston Spa., N. Y. Subsequently he removed to Northampton in the neighboring county of Fulton, then to Milton in Saratoga County, and finally to Verona.

CHILDREN. (*Fourth Generation.*)

*47.   I.   CHLOE, b. Dec. 6, 1785; m. Timothy D. Swan.
*48.   II.   BELDEN, b. June 17, 1787.
*49.   III. JAMES, b. Sept. 20, 1790.
 50.   IV.   JOHN, b. in Ballston, N. Y., May 8, 1792; d in Verona, N. Y., Sept. 4, 1836; m. Deborah Lewis. No children.
*51.   V.   BETSEY, b. Aug. 15, 1794; m. Joel Gray.
 52.   VI.   WILLIAM, b. in Northampton, N. Y., March 30, 1796; d. near Salt Point (Syracuse), N. Y., Oct. 12, 1830. Unmarried.
*53.   VII. TIMOTHY, b. March 15, 1798.
*54.   VIII. JOEL, b. April 5, 1800.
*55.   IX.   ABIGAIL, b. Nov. 7, 1802; m. Abner Stephens.
 56.   X.   NOAH, b. in Milton, N. Y., Nov. 3, 1805; d. in Brighton, N. Y., Sept. 6, 1838. Unmarried.
*57.   XI.   MARY, b. Jan. 12, 1809; m. Aaron Hess.

* These names may not be arranged in correct order of birth.

15.

Daniel Resseguie, born in Ridgefield, May 1, 1760; died in Northampton, Fulton County, N. Y., Feb. 2, 1825. He married (date and place unknown), Mary Monroe, daughter of Capt. David Monroe. She was born in 1763, and died Oct. 21, 1838. Daniel Resseguie resided for a time on Long Island, then in Charlton, N. Y., but about 1790 removed to Northampton (then the town of Broadalbin, Montgomery County), where the remainder of his life was passed. He was a farmer.

CHILDREN. (*Fourth Generation.*)

*58.   I.   DAVID, b. May 19, 1784.
*59.   II.   MARY, b. Jan. 29, 1787; m. Joshua Crouch.
60.   III.   ESTHER, b. March 31, 1788; d. in Northampton, N. Y., Aug. 6, 1844; m. Charles Scott, now deceased. No children.
*61.   IV.   HANNAH MARIAH, b. 1790; m. Spafford Field.
*62.   V.   DANIEL, b. March 9, 1792.
63.   VI.   ALEXANDER, b. 1794; d. 1811.
*64.   VII.   CHARLES, b. Sept. 9, 1797.
*65.   VIII.   SAMUEL, b. Nov. 28, 1800.
*66.   IX.   JACOB, b. Oct. 21, 1803.
*67.   X.   BELDEN, b. May 2, 1806.
68.   XI.   GAYLORD, d. unmarried.
*69.   XII.   MINERVA, b. Feb. 9, 1809; m. Hiram Lewis.

16.

Mary Resseguie, born in 1764; died in Wilton, Conn., Dec. 24, 1848. She was probably the youngest child of Alexander Resseguie, Jr., though by some thought to have been a granddaughter. She was a member of his household, and married, Nov. 28, 1779, Thomas Cole. "He was a soldier of the Revolution, and was with the American army while they were occupying New York city, or Manhattan Island, and the British army were stationed at White Plains. He was taken sick while in the discharge of his duty and released from active service. His wife, inspired with a spirit of patriotism, rode to headquarters from her home in Wilton, on horseback, passing through both the British and American lines, and brought him safely to his home. Receiving an honorable discharge, his widow drew a pension for his services until her death." Mr. Cole died in Wilton.

CHILDREN. (*Fourth Generation.*)

- *70.   I. THOMAS, b. Oct. 22, 1780.
- *71. II. IRA, b. Feb. 10, 1782.
- *72. III. TIMOTHY, b. Aug. 28, 1784.
- *73. IV. SALLY, b. Feb. 9, 1788; m. David Nichols.
- *74.   V. CURTIS, b. May 10, 1790.
- *75. VI. SAMUEL, b. Oct. 22, 1791.
- *76. VII. SHERMAN, b. June 4, 1804.

17.

James Resseguie, born, 1744; died in Ridgefield, Conn., Sept. 7, 1830. He married, Feb. 10, 1766, Sarah Rumsey, who died Oct. 3, 1791. He married (2d) Eunice ———. She died in Ridgefield Dec. 13, 1833, aged 83. The will of James Resseguie was dated Aug. 23, 1823, and presented for probate Oct. 9, 1830. His wife, Eunice, is given the use and improvement of all his estate during her life. To the "heirs of the body of my daughter Sally" he gives $10. To his children Isaac, James, Abraham, Ellen, and Polly, the remainder of his estate after the death of his wife. His "trusty friends," William Keeler and William Hawley of Ridgefield, are appointed executors.

CHILDREN. (*Fourth Generation.*)

- 77.   I. LYMAN, b. Oct. 29, 1766; d. Dec. 18, 1791.
- *78. II. ELLEN, b. Aug. 5, 1767; m. Thomas Mead.
- 79. III. SETH, b. May 19, 1770; probably d. young.
- *80. IV. ISAAC, b. Oct. 7, 1772.
- 81.   V. SALLY, b. ———. Nothing has been learned concerning her beyond the clause in her father's will, bequeathing $10 "to the heirs of the body of my daughter Sally."
- *82. VI. JAMES, b. Jan. 12, 1775.
- *83. VII. ABRAHAM, b. Feb. 6, 1782.
- *84. VIII. POLLY, b. Feb. 21, 1785; m. William Palmer.
- 85.   IX. AARON, b. 1794; d. May 20, 1821.

18.

Sarah Resseguie, married in Ridgefield, Aug. 15, 1771, Seth Bouton of Norwalk, Conn. He was born in 1754, and died Dec. 10, 1840.

CHILDREN. (*Fourth Generation.*)

- 86.   I. PHEBE, b. Dec. 4, 1772.
- 87. II. SARAH, b. July 14, 1778.
- 88. III. SETH, b. Feb. 20, 1780; d. Aug. 27, 1814.

19.

Abraham Resseguie, born in Ridgefield. He married, but the name of his wife is unknown. He removed to Sing Sing, N. Y., and died there. He was a shoemaker by trade. "He was a small, dark-complexioned man, and wore earrings."

CHILDREN. (*Fourth Generation.*)

*89. I.   WILLIAM DAVID, b. Aug. 6, 1792.
 90. II. ABRAHAM, d. in Sing Sing, N. Y., unmarried.
 91. III. JANE, b. ——; m. and has descendants living in Brooklyn, N. Y., but the compiler has been unable to get into communication with them.
*92. IV. SAMUEL, b. 1800.

20.

Abigail Resseguie. The date of her birth is unknown. She married Jesse Nichols, and resided in Rensselaerville, Albany County, N. Y. A brother of Jesse married her sister Hannah. The compiler has tried in vain to connect these brothers with any of the Nichols families of Fairfield County, Conn., where it is known they belonged.

CHILDREN. (*Fourth Generation.*)

*93. I.   JOEL, b. Nov. 11, 1774.
 94. II. JESSE, b. ——. A sailor and lost at sea.
*95. III. SALLY, b. Aug. 9, 1782; m. Asa Phelps.

21.

Jane Resseguie, born in 1750; died Feb. 11, 1823. She married, Feb. 18, 1777, Nathan Smith, son of Samuel and Ruth (Gaylord) Smith, of Ridgefield. He was born July 17, 1753, and died Oct. 1, 1831. They lived in Ridgefield. Mr. Smith represented his town in the State Legislature a number of times.

CHILDREN. (*Fourth Generation.*)

*96.   I.   POLLY, b. Sept. 27, 1778; m. Benjamin Benedict.
 97.   II. ABIGAIL, b. May 7, 1781; d. in Ridgefield, Conn., Nov. 2, 1862; unmarried.
*98.   III. ANNA, b. in Ridgefield, Aug. 1, 1783; m. Jeremiah Dauchey; lived in Troy, N. Y.
*99.   IV. SALLY, b. April 5, 1786; m. Thaddeus Jewett.
*100. V.   NATHAN, b. Nov. 11, 1788.

22.

Rachel Resseguie, born in Norwalk, Conn., April 11, 1752; died in Danbury, Conn., Jan. 31, 1839. She married, May 18, 1775, John Peck, who was born in Danbury, Sept. 10, 1747, and died there, Nov. 13, 1804. She was a woman who possessed a lively disposition, full of strength and energy, while her husband was of an easy and good-natured temperament. They were considered well mated.

CHILDREN. (*Fourth Generation.*)

*101.   I.   HANNAH, b. Aug. 15, 1776; m. Eli Gregory.
 102.   II. RACHEL RESSEGUIE, b. June 6, 1778; d. in Danbury, Conn., Oct., 1863; unmarried.
*103.   III. REBECKAH, b. March 20, 1783; m. Eli Mygatt.
*104.   IV. JOHN MORRIS, b. Oct. 7, 1786.
*105.   V.   THOMAS RESSEGUIE, b. April 3, 1792.

23.

Phebe Resseguie, born March 31, 1754; died in New Milford, Conn., Feb. 9, 1815. She married, June 25, 1778, Asa Prime, son of William and Sarah (Garlick) Prime of New Milford, where he was born July 15, 1753, and died April 6, 1817. Asa Prime was a blacksmith, and was employed during Revolutionary times in making the chain which was stretched across the Hudson River to prevent the passage of the British fleet. He was a very athletic man and a skilled wrestler, and was victorious in New York, Philadelphia, and Baltimore, whither he went for trials of skill and strength with others.

CHILDREN. (*Fourth Generation.*)

*106.   I.   WILLIAM, b. June 7, 1779.
*107.   II. PHEBE, b. May 4, 1781; m. Abel Canfield, Jr.
*108.   III. JANE, b. Nov. 11, 1782; m. Samuel Treadwell.
*109.   IV. ASA, b. Nov. 16, 1791.

24.

Hannah Resseguie, born in Ridgefield, May 9, 1757; died in Fenner, Madison County, N. Y., Nov. 21, 1827. She married in Ridgefield, July 23, 1777, Samuel Nichols, whose brother Jesse married her sister Abigail. He was born in Norwalk, Conn., Jan. 9, 1758, and died Dec. 18, 1849, aged 92 years. He removed from Connecticut to Rensselaerville, N. Y., soon after the Revolution, and to the Mile Strip, Fenner (then Cazenovia), in 1802. " He was a man of extraordinary vigor and energy, maintaining his strength until within the last three years, having scarcely ever known what it was to be sick. He entered the army at the commencement of the war, at the age of 16, and served to its close, — seven years and five months, when he was discharged honorably by General Washington himself. At the battle of Monmouth he received a musket ball in the leg which he carried in his flesh for seventy-two years; after his death, and at his own previous request, it was extracted and is now in the possession of the family. He was a faithful son of liberty in his youth, a good citizen and father during his manhood, and a devout Christian for fifty years." He was a trustee in the Presbyterian Church, town superintendent of the poor, assessor, and inspector of elections, conducting all offices to the full satisfaction of his constituency. He married (2d), April 10, 1828, Mrs. Sybil Cranson, who was born March 17, 1764.

CHILDREN. (*Fourth Generation.*)

*110.   I.   SAMUEL, b. Oct. 5, 1779.
*111. II.   LUCINDA, b. June 24, 1781; m. Moses Rice.
*112. III.   ANNIS, b. Oct. 18, 1783; m. Peter Love.
*113. IV.   HANNAH, b. Aug. 14, 1785; m. Jacob Bump.
 114.   V.   HENRY, b. Nov. 24, 1787; d. June 26, 1789.
 115. VI.   CLARISSA, b. Nov. 24, 1787; d. Feb. 5, 1788.
*116. VII.   HARRY, b. Feb. 1, 1789.
 117. VIII. ABRAHAM RESSEGUIE, b. Feb. 5, 1792; d. Jan. 6, 1812.
*118. IX.   WILLIAM, b. May 14, 1795.
 119.   X.   POLLY, b. Sept. 15, 1797; d. Jan. 15, 1798.
 120. XI.   MATILDA, b. April 8, 1799; d. April 4, 1811.
*121. XII.   HARVEY RESSEGUIE, b. May 9, 1802.

25.

John Resseguie, born in Ridgefield, April 2, 1758; died in Sharon, N. Y., May 9, 1840. He married, Nov. 20, 1783, Anna Camp, who was born Oct. 9, 1761, and died June 11, 1788. He married (2d), Jan. 17, 1789, Abigail Brailey, who was born May 16, 1754, and died June 28, 1808. He married (3d), April 18, 1809, Mrs. Anna (Thompson) McDonald, born June 8, 1770, and died Sept. 21, 1844.

Mr. Resseguie served for three years as a soldier in the Revolutionary war. He was a private in the Fourth Westchester County Regiment, commanded by Col. Thomas Crane. He was captured by the British, June 24, 1779, and released on the 14th of August. At another time he barely escaped capture by swimming to a boat in the Hudson River, losing his musket in the effort. He settled in Sharon, Schoharie County, N. Y., in the year 1795, after a short stay at Rensselaerville, and passed the remainder of his life in that town, engaged in farming.

CHILDREN. (*Fourth Generation.*)

*122. I. NATHANIEL, b. Oct. 8, 1784.
*123. II. MARY, b. Aug. 28, 1786; m. Aldrich W. Barrett.
*124. III. ANNA, b. May 10, 1788; m. Robert Mitchell.
*125. IV. PHŒBE, b. June 25, 1792; m. James Phelps.
*126. V. JOHN, b. May 17, 1793.
*127. VI. ELIZABETH, b. May 30, 1795; m. Samuel V. Way.

26.

Mary Resseguie, born April 17, 1747; married David Burt. By her father's will, made March 13, 1799, she was to receive five shillings. The compiler has been unable to learn anything further concerning her.

CHILDREN. (*Fourth Generation.*)

128. I. SEABORN. (Born at sea.)
129. II. BETSEY.
130. III. HANNAH.
131. IV. DAVID.

27.

Jacob Resseguie, born June 5, 1752; died July 24, 1835. He married, April 14, 1780, Sarah Folliot, who died June 27, 1827, aged 78 years. He served a short time in the Revolutionary war, and afterwards sent a substitute. He lived in Ridgefield, Conn., and was a farmer.

CHILDREN. (*Fourth Generation.*)

*132. I. BETSEY, b. June, 1781; m. Alpheus Canfield.
133. II. SAMUEL, b. about 1785; died in Indiana (then a Territory), July 18, 1815; unmarried.
*134. III. ABIJAH, b. March 26, 1791.

135. IV. RALPH, b. ——. At the breaking out of the war of the Rebellion he was in Texas, and has not since been heard from. He was unmarried.
136. V. ALEXANDER, d. young.

29.

Alexander Resseguie, born in Ridgefield, May 24, 1759; died there Dec. 28, 1835. He married in Ridgefield, Ruhamah Keeler, born in that town Aug. 16, 1768, and died there Dec. 17, 1859, aged 91 years.

CHILDREN. (*Fourth Generation.*)

*137. I. ELIZA, b. May 7, 1800; m. Nelson Hallock.
138. II. LEWIS, b. in Ridgefield, Conn., 1806; d. there, June 26, 1834.

FOURTH GENERATION.

31.

James Riggs, born June 29, 1765; died Feb. 9, 1854. He married, Jan. 22, 1789, Sarah Miles, daughter of Stephen and Mary (Gunn) Miles of New Milford, Conn., who was born Aug. 15, 1770, and died April 15, 1853. They lived in Sherman, Conn.

CHILDREN. (*Fifth Generation.*)

139.	I.	STEPHEN, b. Sept. 13, 1790; d. Feb. 20, 1871; m. Minerva Stone, who died Feb. 22, 1874. They lived in Poughquag, N. Y.
140.	II.	ALTA, b. Nov. 2, 1792; d. May 19, 1828; m. March 15, 1821. Isaac Hine of New Milford, b. June 23, 1791; d. Oct. 4, 1873.
141.	III.	ANN, b. Jan. 27, 1795; d. Sept. 12, 1876; m. April 24, 1828, Thomas Hall of Sherman, Conn., b. Aug. 26, 1790; d. March 17, 1871.
142.	IV.	JOSEPH MILES, b. Feb. 9, 1797; d. Feb. 27, 1844; m. Daphne Holmes.
143.	V.	JAMES WOOSTER, b. Aug. 13, 1799; d. Aug. 18, 1838; m. in 1828, Mary Ann DeReemer, b. Dec. 7, 1803.
144.	VI.	PHEBE MARGARET, b. March 27, 1803; d. March 11, 1880; m. 1830, Benjamin Briggs of Pawling, N. Y., b. Dec. 6, 1793.
145.	VII.	ISAAC, b. Aug. 18, 1805; d. April 4, 1839; m. Nov. 30, 1828, Cornelia Louisa Leach, b. Jan. 24, 1809; d. April 3, 1840.
146.	VIII.	LAURA CANDACE, b. May 8, 1808; m. Feb. 20, 1839, Peter Francis LeRoy, b. Dec. 11, 1808. Both reside in Rochester, Mich.
147.	IX.	ELIJAH BELDEN, b. Nov. 2, 1810; d. Oct. 5, 1814.

32.

Miles Riggs, born in Norwalk, Conn., Sept. 10, 1767; died May 12, 1840. He married, Aug. 10, 1791, Mrs. Suse Patchin,* who was born in Norwalk May 19, 1766, and died Sept. 2, 1857. About 1790 Mr. Riggs removed to Ballston, N. Y., and in 1802, or the following year, to Groton, Tompkins County, where he

---

* Mrs. Patchin's maiden name was Taylor. Her husband, with a party of surveyors, were on or near the Muskingum River, Ohio, when they were attacked by Indians, and all but one killed.

purchased fifty acres of land. The country was new and covered with heavy forests, and the work of clearing a farm was an arduous task. Subsequently Mr. Riggs became the owner of a farm of 640 acres, or a mile square. He was a musician, and soon after getting settled in his new home was invited by the miller, on whom he was dependent for his mill work, to bring his fiddle along when he came to mill. He did so, and played vigorously while the grist was being ground. After the flour was placed in the wagon the miller said: "I have not tolled your grist, Mr. Riggs. Now, any time you want grinding done you come and fiddle for me, and I will grind for you." And for years he fiddled out his grist work. A few years after his death his widow removed to Plainfield, N. J., and died there.

Mr. Riggs was an austere, dignified man, but had also a vein of humor in his composition. On one occasion Deacon Daniel Bradley of Groton came along, after a hard day's work at clearing land, and challenged Mr. Riggs to fiddle for him as long as he would dance. The challenge was accepted, and the deacon was obliged to "tread the light fantastic toe" until the next morning. At one time his services as musician brought him 1,000 feet of clear pine lumber, which he contributed to the new meeting house, then in process of construction, and it was made into a pulpit. Mr. Riggs was an Episcopalian, but attended the Presbyterian church, then the only one in Groton. His old log house was kept as a tavern, and Mrs. Riggs was a famous landlady. Her excellent table and beds attracted all regular travelers, who made it a point to spend a night there. In 1824 Mr. Riggs built the largest dwelling house in the town, where his children and their families often met, to the number of thirty or forty. On one of his visits to Albany he purchased a cooking stove, which was the first one used in the town of Groton. He is remembered as a strictly just man, always sincerely honest in his dealings and requiring the same of others.

CHILDREN. (*Fifth Generation.*)

148.   I.   IRA, b. May 7, 1792; d. March 3, 1874; m. March 19, 1819, Sally Bradley, b. Dec. 17, 1794; d. June 21, 1865. m. (2d) Mrs. Adeline S. Grant. They lived at Kings Ferry, N. Y.

149.   II. LEWIS, b. Nov. 14, 1793; d. April 7, 1839; m. Jan. 25, 1821, Lydia Childs, b. July 29, 1802; and resides in Waverly, Ia.

150.	III.	ZENAS, b. Jan. 26, 1796; d. April 13, 1869; m. April 11, 1820, Susan Angeline Blakeley, b. April 6, 1794; d. Nov. 19, 1871. They lived at Candor, N. Y.
151.	IV.	LAURA, b. Jan. 1, 1798; d. Nov. 6, 1844; m. Oct. 3, 1826, Moses Lyon, b. April 2, 1790; d. Feb. 27, 1874.
152.	V.	ALFRED, b. June 20, 1800; d. Nov. 24, 1871; m. Oct. 13, 1828, Abigail Watson Tyler, b. Nov. 25, 1801; d. Aug. 26, 1882.
153.	VI.	HORACE ALEXANDER, b. Nov. 16, 1802; m. Jan. 30, 1831, Abigail Dudley Morse, b. March 5, 1793; d. Feb. 15, 1860. m. (2d) Sept. 10, 1862, Mrs. Nancy Celestia Bingham, née Seymour. They reside in Plymouth, O.
154.	VII.	GEORGE, b. Feb. 15, 1806; d. Feb. 20, 1880; m. April 15, 1832, Maria Powers, b. April 3, 1809; d. Oct. 3, 1873. m. (2d) May 5, 1874, Mrs. Kate Hills.
155.	VIII.	MARILDA SUSAN, b. June 12, 1809; d. May 29, 1875.

34.

Timothy Riggs, born Oct. 29, 1772; died at East Line, Saratoga County, N. Y., Sept. 14, 1848. He married, in Milton, N. Y., Oct. 27, 1796, Candace Weed, daughter of John and Hannah Weed of New Hampshire. She was born in that State Sept. 8, 1779, and died in Malta, N. Y., May 12, 1853. Mr. Riggs was a farmer, and resided at East Line.

CHILDREN. (*Fifth Generation.*)

156.	I.	MATILDA, b. Nov. 8, 1797; d. Sept. 25, 1842; m. Oct. 9, 1816, Timothy Marvin, b. Nov. 24, 1792; d. Jan. 1, 1847.
157.	II.	MINERVA, b. Aug. 12, 1799; d. Sept. 21, 1842; m. 1819, Joseph Wagner, Jr., who died at Fort Plain, N. Y.
158.	III.	ELI, b. Aug. 28, 1802; d. Sept. 13, 1859; m. Sept. 21, 1827, Mary Eunice Soules, b. Oct. 1, 1808; d. March 8, 1872. They lived in Saline, Mich.
159.	IV.	JOHN WEED, b. Aug. 26, 1804; d. July 21, 1873; m. Oct. 24, 1825, Maria Philipena Gros; b. Jan. 28, 1804; d. July 22, 1886. They resided at St. Johnsville, N. Y.
160.	V.	ALFRED, b. Oct. 8, 1806; d. April 6, 1852; m. Sept. 18, 1827, Esther Romer, b. Jan. 10, 1810. She resides in New York.
161.	VI.	EMELINE, b. Nov. 8, 1808; d. March 12, 1822.
162.	VII.	JOSEPH, b. June 3, 1811; d. July 2, 1877; m. Oct. 3, 1837, Alida Beekman, b. June 27, 1815. He lived in Detroit, Mich.
163.	VIII.	HANNAH MARGARET, b. July 21, 1813; d. Oct. 9, 1813.
164.	IX.	MARGARET HANNAH, b. July 21, 1813; d. June 24, 1814.
165.	X.	HANNAH MARGARET, b. Jan. 17, 1817; m. Nov. 9, 1842, John Munson Olmstead, b. Sept. 17, 1811; d. Sept. 8, 1875. She resides in Albany, N. Y.
166.	XI.	JAMES, b. April 22, 1819; d. Nov. 18, 1835.

167. XII. FRANCES EMELINE, b. Feb. 22, 1823; d. Nov. 22, 1846; m. Harvey Eliphalet Williams, b. June 17, 1808; d. Nov. 18, 1871. They lived at Fort Plain, N. Y.
168. XIII. HIRAM TIMOTHY, b. Aug. 21, 1825; d. July 18, 1856.
169. XIV. WILLIAM HENRY, b. March 27, 1828; resides in Lincoln, Neb.

35.

Sarah Riggs, born May 6, 1778; died in West Troy, N. Y., Feb. 24, 1870. She married in Ballston, N. Y., Nov., 1798, Raymond Taylor, who was born in Connecticut, Feb. 19, 1770, and died in West Troy, Dec. 23, 1851. He was a mechanic.

CHILDREN. (*Fifth Generation.*)

170. I. HARRY R., b. Aug. 16, 1799; d. Jan. 15, 1866; m. Nov. 11, 1847, Mrs. Anna E. Hochstrasser, b. Dec. 1, 1822; d. Feb. 26, 1860.
171. II. CAROLINE, b. May 8, 1801; d. June 18, 1838; m. Feb. 22, 1825, Clark Salisbury, b. Oct. 12, 1797; d. April 12, 1875.
172. III. MINNETTA, b. April 27, 1804; d. Sept. 6, 1869.
173. IV. MORGAN LEWIS, b. May 18, 1806; m. Sept. 22, 1842, Maria Lobdell, b. July 17, 1812; d. July 29, 1843. He resides in West Troy, N. Y.
174. V. JAMES BRISBIN, b. June 5, 1818; d. May 20, 1869; m. Oct. 18, 1863, Matilda Withers Dunham, b. May 23, 1836. She resides in St. Augustine, Fla.

39.

Alexander Resseguie, born April 18, 1777; died July 7, 1858. He married Eunice Meaker, daughter of Jared and Mabel (Cole) Meaker. She was born June 12, 1775, and died Dec. 16, 1842. They removed from Connecticut to Hubbardton, Vt., in 1802, thence to Benson in the same State about the year 1815.

CHILDREN. (*Fifth Generation.*)

175. I. DANIEL MEAKER, b. April 18, 1797; d. Jan. 8, 1866; m. March 3, 1850, Ruby Walker. She m. (2d), Dec. 29, 1868, Horace A. Seymour, and resides in Leicester, Vt.
176. II. ESTHER, b. Oct. 29, 1799; d. Dec. 26, 1882; m. Jan. 1824, James Hubbard Gleason, b. April 27, 1799; d. Aug. 26, 1883. They resided in Benson, Vt.
177. III. ELIZABETH, b. Nov. 22, 1802; d. Feb. 27, 1884; m. Feb. 9, 1826, George Edward Parmalee, b. March 12, 1797; d. Nov. 10, 1884. They lived in Morris, Ill.
178. IV. NABBY, b. Nov. 8, 1803; d. Feb. 8, 1813.

179.   v.   JOHN, b. Dec. 23, 1804; d. Dec. 2, 1847; m. Nov. 24, 1831, Emeline Sheldon. She resides in St. Charles, Ill.
180.   vi.   HARRY, b. March 19, 1806; d. Nov. 22, 1859; m. June 3, 1835, Betsey Sheldon, sister of his brother John's wife, b. Sept. 28, 1811; d. Jan. 11, 1884.
181.   vii. DAVID, b. Dec. 18, 1808; d. Feb. 1813.
182.   viii. EUNICE MARIA, b. March 25, 1810; d. Dec. 10, 1884; m. March 10, 1830, Ozias Bissell Herrick. He resides in Joliet, Ill.
183.   ix.   JULIA ANN, b. Sept. 11, 1811; d. Oct. 15, 1828.
184.   x.   ALEXANDER, b. June 7, 1812; m. Oct. 28, 1835, Betsey Merriam, who d. March 21, 1857. m. (2d), Feb. 22, 1866, Orlinda Adnelro Riford. They reside in Rutland, Vt.
185.   xi.   PERMELIA, b. March 24, 1814; m. Sept. 1, 1831, Wilson Alvin Proctor, b. June 20, 1810; d. Aug. 4, 1873. She resides in Castleton, Vt.
186.   xii. ALPHEUS ALONZO, b. Sept. 12, 1816; d. Jan. 24, 1883; m. Jan. 1, 1845, Mary Walker, twin sister of his brother Daniel's wife. She resides in Franklin, Mass. Mr. Resseguie changed the orthography of the name in his family to *Ressegue*.
187.   xiii. GEORGE FORDICE, b. July 8, 1818; m. Jan. 1, 1838, Mary Ann Felton. They reside in Warrenville, Ill.

40.

William Resseguie. (No dates can be found.) He married near Albany, N. Y., Catharine Secor. They lived in the town of Fishkill, N. Y., where he died when his children were young. His widow married Clark Stone, as his second wife, and died in Stormville, town of Fishkill.

CHILDREN. (*Fifth Generation.*)

188.   i.   SUSAN, b. about 1797; d. Feb. 1834; m. Gilbert Sutton, who d. 1826. m. (2d) William Rozell, who d. about 1857.
189.   ii.   JOHN, m.; had no children.
190.   iii. LYMAN, d. unmarried.
191.   iv.   ANN, m. Edward Poole, a sea captain. No children.
192.   v.   NOAH, b. Dec. 10, 1809; m. Ellen Vredenburg, b. Feb. 19, 1811; d. July 15, 1882. He spells his name *Rusky*, and resides (1886) at Crafts, N. Y.
193.   vi.   WILLIAM, b. 1811; d. Aug. 16, 1839; m. Aug. 28, 1834, Lydia Denton, who m. (2d), Dec. 8, 1843, John Dyson. She resides in Reedsburgh, Wis.
194.   vii. CHARLOTTE, b. April 6, 1812; d. Jan. 18, 1863; m. Jan. 2, 1826, John MacKinnon, b. May 4, 1800; d. Aug. 18, 1864.
195.   viii. MARY AMELIA, b. April 6, 1812; d. Nov. 1851; m. 1835, Charles Louis Gereaux, b. 1815; d. April 19, 1847.

41.

Stephen Resseguie, born in 1774; died Nov. 13, 1863. He married Sarah Barrett, who was born in 1776, and died Sept. 6, 1834. He married (2d) Nancy Barrett, who is not now living. Stephen Resseguie settled in the town of Kent, Putnam County, N. Y., on the east shore of White Pond, about two miles from the village of Farmers Mills, formerly known as "Milltown." He was a farmer.

CHILDREN. (*Fifth Generation.*)

196.	I.	Isaac, b. March 28, 1808; d. Aug. 4, 1877; m. Sept. 3, 1828, Mary Robinson (239), b. 1812; d. Aug. 31, 1885.
197.	II.	Belden, m. and "went west."
198.	III.	Melissa, d. young.
199.	IV.	Laura, m. Caleb Davis. Both dead.
200.	V.	Samuel, b. April 1, 1819; m. Feb. 1, 1846, Semantha Patrick. Resides in Farmers Mills, N. Y.
201.	VI.	Deborah, b. Nov. 22, 1821; m. Jan. 16, 1839, Elvin Mead, b. Sept. 16, 1819. They reside at Farmers Mills, N. Y.
202.	VII.	Mary, d. young.
203.	VIII.	Noah, b. May 8, 1828; d. May 12, 1867; m. Dec. 20, 1853, Esther M. Carpenter, who d. May 28, 1873.
204.	IX.	William, b. 1841; m. 1856, Sarah Jane Worden. They reside at Farmers Mills, N. Y.
205.	X.	Alexander, d. in childhood.

42.

Noah Resseguie. He removed to Susquehanna County, Pennsylvania, remaining there but a short time, however, when he went to New York State and settled in Milo, Yates County. He married Mary Reynolds. About 1840 the family removed to Bloom, Logan County, Ohio. The dates of death of Noah and his wife have not been ascertained, but he is said to have "died suddenly one day while in the milk-yard."

CHILDREN. (*Fifth Generation.*)

206.	I.	Malinda, m. about 1833, Thomas Lee.
207.	II.	Jesse, b. about 1819; d. May 11, 1840.

43.

Samuel Resseguie, born in Ridgefield, March 12, 1776; died in South Gibson, Pa., Sept. 12, 1858. He married in Westport, Conn., Nov. 2, 1797, Freelove Disbrow, daughter of Justus[*] and Elizabeth (Sherwood) Disbrow of that place. She died in South Gibson, April 28, 1830, aged 49 years. He married (2d) in Clifford, Pa., June 22, 1831, Nabby Pickering Miller, widow of David Miller and daughter of Jotham[†] and Elsie (Pickering) Pickering of Clifford. She was born May 4, 1786, and died in Lenox, Pa., March 27, 1867.

Samuel Resseguie resided in several different places in the vicinity of Fishkill, N. Y., until about 1806, when he purchased a farm near what is now called Farmers Mills, Putnam County, where he remained until his emigration to Pennsylvania, where he arrived May 8, 1813. He settled in what is now South Gibson in Susquehanna County, on wild land situated in the valley of the Tunkhannock, one of the principal tributaries of the Susquehanna River. Here he endured the hardships and suffered the privations of a pioneer life, in common with the early settlers of Gibson township (the principal part of whom originally came from Connecticut). His wife, Freelove, is described as possessing a small, lithe figure, energetic, industrious, and in every way a prudent helpmate, manufacturing with her own hands from the raw flax and wool the wherewithal to clothe her family. After the lapse of seventeen years, when the log cabin had been supplanted by the "framed house," and the wilderness was fast receding before the approach of civilization, at the dawn of better days, she was summoned to lay down her life work.

---

[*] Justus Disbrow was a soldier of the Revolutionary War. While absent from his home, engaged in the defense of his country, his wife, who was left with eight children to provide for, heard that "the Tories were coming," and carried her beds, clothing, and provisions and hid them in the swamp, but they were discovered and burned together with the house and all it contained. The affrighted mother and children sought refuge behind a stone hog-pen, which was battered by the bullets of the enemy, who, on discovering the hidden family, tore the clothing off the children's backs and cast it into the fire.

[†] Jotham Pickering emigrated with his family in 1793, from Mendon, Mass., to New Milford, Pa., "and removed to Gibson in 1798, that he might unite his family of children with those of another to establish the first school in Gibson township." It is related in the history of Susquehanna County that the first teacher in Gibson did not know how to write. Mr. Pickering and his family figure largely in the history of the county. The youngest son of Mrs. Miller, Dr. A. P. Miller, became an efficient school teacher and practitioner of medicine, and was the first postmaster of South Gibson, which position he retained until his death. Her daughter married a son of Samuel Resseguie (Lewis 213) and her son Henry's children have married into the Resseguie family.

In personal appearance Samuel Resseguie was a type of foreign blood, his father being of French and his mother of Irish descent. He possessed perfect health, never being obliged to call a physician until his last sickness. His sanguine temperament, florid complexion, and great obesity rendered him fair, fat, and funny. Physically he bore a striking resemblance to Sir John Falstaff. His corpulence and longevity were transmitted to nearly all his children. That he had strength of character is evidenced by the fact of his signing the pledge during a Washingtonian temperance movement, which he preserved inviolate to the day of his death, which occurred some twenty-five or thirty years later. Politically he was a Democrat, until the formation of the Republican party, the slavery question causing him to forsake the one and embrace the other. The history of Napoleon Bonaparte, and his old family Bible (weighing eighteen pounds), were his chosen library and chief companions during his declining years.

CHILDREN. (*Fifth Generation.*)

208. I. BETSEY ELIZABETH, b. July 12, 1798; d. Nov. 30, 1876; m. 1817, George Conrad, b. Dec. 22, 1794; d. Nov. 5, 1856.
209. II. SARAH, b. Sept. 25, 1800; d. Jan. 18, 1876; m. Aug. 1830, Walter Dickey, who d. May, 1861.
210. III. CYNTHIA, b. Dec. 12, 1802; d. July 25, 1883; m. June 23, 1834, George Washington Starks, who d. Nov. 26, 1875.
211. IV. FITCH PATRICK, b. Feb. 13, 1805; m. Oct. 23, 1832, Mary Tewksbury, b. Aug. 17, 1813; d. April 28, 1876. He resides in South Gibson, Pa.
212. V. AARON, b. Aug. 17, 1807; m. Jan. 23, 1831, Betsey Ann Denney, who d. March 3, 1884. He resides in South Gibson.
213. VI. LEWIS, b. Feb. 25, 1810; d. Jan. 13, 1879; m. Nov. 15, 1831, Nabby Ann Miller, who d. June 11, 1853; m. (2d), Aug. 21, 1853, Mary Elizabeth Martin, who d. March 1, 1855; m. (3d), April 29, 1855, Mrs. Abigail (Lathrop) Graves, who resides in Berlin, Wis.
214. VII. HARRISON, b. Feb. 1, 1813; resides at South Gibson, Pa., unmarried.
215. VIII. WILLIAM, b. Oct. 28, 1816; d. Sept. 24, 1844; m. March 4, 1836, Jemima Comstock, who d. July 19, 1884.
216. IX. NELSON MANLEY, b. Feb. 21, 1821; m. Oct. 25, 1846, Eliza Ann Tripp. They reside in Clifford, Pa.

44.

Sarah Resseguie. (No dates can be found.) She is said to have been married (1st) to Riley Ganung, by whom she had children. They removed from Connecticut to the "Lake country" of New York. She married (2d) David Coon. There were no children by this marriage. She married (3d) William Botsford, and lived with him at Little Falls, also at Quality Hill, Madison County, N. Y. She died in Canada. Mr. Botsford was formerly a sea captain and afterwards a shoemaker. He died at Quality Hill.

CHILDREN. (*Fifth Generation.*)

217. I. HENRY BOTSFORD, b. Jan. 9, 1800; d. May 14, 1841; m. Feb. 12, 1823, Charlotte Thayer, b. Oct. 17, 1805; d. Feb. 15, 1886.
218. II. ELIZA BOTSFORD, b. Nov. 9, 1800; d. May 25, 1869; m. July 16, 1819, Simon Allen, b. Dec. 28, 1798. Resides in Lyndonville, N. Y.

45.

Susan Resseguie, born in Ridgefield, Conn., April 18, 1796; died in Greenwood, Steuben County, N. Y., April 30, 1878. She married in Fishkill, N. Y., Aug. 7, 1812, Jeremiah Whitney, who was born in Fishkill, June 17, 1787, and died at Chatham, Pa., Aug. 4, 1867. Mr. Whitney was a shoemaker. They lived in various places, including Fishkill, Milo, Beekman, Reading, and Tyrone, all in New York, and Bingham and Chatham in Pennsylvania. (See *Whitney Genealogy*.)

CHILDREN. (*Fifth Generation.*)

219. I. JOYCE, b. May 18, 1813; d. April 10, 1872; m. May 28, 1833, Hiram Merrick. He resides in West Bingham, Pa.
220. II. MINERVA, b. July 6, 1814; d. March 10, 1824.
221. III. WILLIAM LEWIS, b. Sept. 29, 1816; m. Dec. 21, 1842, Adeline Cook, b. March 17, 1826; d. April 15, 1884. He resides in Middlebury, Pa.
222. IV. SARAH ANN, b. Oct. 29, 1817; m. Dec. 21, 1838, Dahyler Brown. Residence, Hayes City, Kan.
223. V. JEREMIAH, b. Feb. 10, 1819; m. June 9, 1844, Sarah Goodwin, b. May 27, 1824. They live in Andover, N. Y.
224. VI. CAROLINE, b. Nov. 10, 1820; d. Jan. 11, 1877; m. May 1, 1837, Lester Merrick. They reside in Chatham, Pa.
225. VII. ELIAS, b. Sept. 1, 1822; m. June 19, 1850, Laurette Short, who d. May 17, 1875. His residence is Chatham, Pa.
226. VIII. SUSAN, b. Feb. 28, 1824; m. March 1, 1847, Charles Sweet. Residence, Middlebury.
227. IX. PHEBE, b. Nov. 6, 1825; d. Feb. 6, 1855.
228. X. SUNILDA, b. Aug. 14, 1827; m. May 11, 1844, Horatio Seymour Keeney. Residence, Middlebury.

229. XI. JOSEPH, b. Feb. 15, 1830; m. Oct. 11, 1855, Julia Spencer. They reside in Middlebury.
230. XII. POLLY, b. Nov. 6, 1831; m. March 18, 1853, Alonzo Button. Residence, Chatham.
231. XIII. RILEY, b. May 20, 1833; m. Oct. 12, 1856, Mary Lizette Short, b. Feb. 28, 1837. They live in Middlebury.
232. XIV. DELILAH, b. Aug 17, 1834; m. Oct. 4, 1854, Francis Short. Residence, Chatham.
233. XV. FITCH, b. May 27, 1837; m. July 4, 1857, Sally Ann Spencer. Residence, Sandusky, N. Y.
234. XVI. NEWBERRY, b. April 29, 1839; m. Aug. 12, 1861, Annette Edwards. They reside in Greenwood, N. Y.

46.

Thankful Resseguie. (No dates.) Married Ebenezer Robinson. They resided in Putnam County, N. Y. (probably near Farmers Mills), where they both died.

CHILDREN. (*Fifth Generation*)

235. I. SUSAN, b. about 1801; d. Oct. 16, 1874; m. James Ager.
236. II. LUCY, b. Dec. 23, 1803; m. Oct., 1821, George Raymond, Jr., who d. Jan. 25, 1876. She resides in Lodi Center, N. Y.
237. III. DAVID, m. Almira Disbrow. Both dead.
238. IV. BETHIA, d. unmarried.
239. V. MARY, b. 1812; d. Aug. 31, 1885; m. Sept. 3, 1828, Isaac Resseguie (196), b. March 28, 1808; d. Aug. 4, 1877.
240. VI. MORRIS, d. 1882, unmarried.
241. VII. SARAH. Resides in Bridgeport, Conn.
242. VIII. EBENEZER, b. 1815; d. Nov. 12, 1863; m. 1840, Fannie Ketura Disbrow, b. 1823. She m. (2d) James Turner; resides in Danbury, Conn.
243. IX. ROSELLA, b. 1822; d. June 25, 1868; m. 1846, Albert Gordon Weaver, b. March 7, 1827. He resides in Marcellus, N. Y.

47.

Chloe Resseguie, born in Ridgefield, Conn., Dec. 6, 1785; died in Spring township, Crawford County, Pa., June 28, 1849. She married Timothy Dwight Swan, who was born in Stonington, Conn., Oct. 17, 1774, and died in Durhamville, Oneida County, N. Y., April 10, 1848. Mr. Swan was the great-uncle of General Ulysses S. Grant. At the time of his marriage he was a resident of Milton, Saratoga County, N. Y., but afterwards removed to Verona, N. Y. He was a chairmaker.

CHILDREN. (*Fifth Generation.*)

244. I. ELIAS LEE, b. June 9, 1806; d. Nov. 13, 1808.
245. II. TIMOTHY DWIGHT, b. July 3, 1807; disappeared.
246. III. HIRAM RESSEGUIE, b. Nov. 12, 1808; d. July, 1876; m. Nov. 12, 1830, Amanda Melinda Scriven, b. May 5, 1806; d. June 23, 1860.
247. IV. MARY ANN, b. Nov. 17, 1810; d. April 20, 1881; m. April 14, 1835, Major Gay Penfield. He resides in Waukon, Iowa.
248. V. JEFFERSON LEE, b. March 13, 1812; m. March 10, 1844, Mrs. Almira (Brockway) Cone. Residence, Caneadea, N. Y.
249. VI. DEMISE, b. Feb. 18, 1815; d. 1833.
250. VII. ELIAS ANDREW, b. Feb. 14, 1818; m. Oct. 14, 1851, Adelia Bailey. Residence, Waukon, Iowa.

48.

Belden Resseguie, born in Ridgefield, Conn., June 17, 1787; died in Van Buren, Onondaga County, N. Y., Aug. 31, 1868. He married, Feb. 11, 1810, Lucy Avery, daughter of Punderson and Levina (Barnes) Avery of Pompey, N. Y. She was born March 14, 1791, and died in Van Buren, March 9, 1841. They commenced housekeeping in 1811, in Verona, but in 1814 removed to Rome, to Pompey in 1817, and in 1820 to Camillus, Onondaga County, and when the town was divided in 1828, found themselves in the new town of Van Buren. Mr. Resseguie served as first lieutenant in the war of 1812, and took part in the battles of Oswego and Sackett's Harbor, and was honorably discharged at the close of the war, which was just before his removal to Rome. He was Assessor of the town of Van Buren for twenty-eight years, and Supervisor four years. He was a very successful farmer, and amassed a handsome property. Of a charitable disposition he lent a helping hand to many, and died greatly lamented by all.

CHILDREN. (*Fifth Generation.*)

251. I. GEORGE, b. Oct. 23, 1811; m. Feb. 26, 1832, Rachel Eaton, who d. Aug. 2, 1843; m. (2d) Oct. 23, 1843, Matilda Mann, who d. Aug. 8, 1844; m. (3d) April 5, 1845, Amelia Brown, who d. March 3, 1884. Residence, Ridgeway, N. Y.
252. II. LORETTA, b. May 13, 1818; m. Jan. 1, 1839, Amasa Philip Hart, b. Sept. 28, 1814. They reside in Phœnix, N. Y.
253. III. WILLIAM, b. May 15, 1823; m. Sept. 19, 1844, Laura Hart. They reside in Grand Ledge, Mich.
254. IV. LEVINA, b. June 20, 1827; m. Jan. 15, 1845, Hiram Stephen Larkin, who d. Sept. 27, 1875. She resides in Van Buren, N. Y.

49.

James Resseguie, born in Ballston, N. Y., Sept. 20, 1790; died in Tuolumne County, Cal., March 13, 1850. He married, Dec. 7, 1817, Lydia Meigs Leete, daughter of Noah and Huldah (Ward) Leete of Verona, N. Y., but formerly of Connecticut. She died in Buffalo, N. Y., March 14, 1864. Their home was in Verona.

CHILDREN. (*Fifth Generation.*)

255.	I.	MARIA EMILY, b. Dec. 6, 1818; d. Sept. 15, 1857; m. Oct. 11, 1838, Joseph Harden, b. March 3, 1815. He resides in Marion, N. Y.
256.	II.	EMILY AMANDA, b. July 14, 1820; m. Nov. 3, 1841, William Nash Peckham. They live in Verona, N. Y.
257.	III.	HARLEY LEETE, b. Feb. 12, 1822; d. Aug. 12, 1844.
258.	IV.	CAROLINE AMELIA, b. Dec. 30, 1823; m. Dec. 23, 1844, James Vroman, who d. July 29, 1868. She resides in Buffalo, N. Y.
259.	V.	HENRY CLAY, b. Jan. 2, 1826; m. Angenette Barber, who d. Nov. 29, 1876.
260.	VI.	MARY ADALINE, b. Feb. 24, 1828; d. Dec. 22, 1856; m. Dec. 23, 1846, Thomas M. Shattuck. He lives in Forestville, N. Y.
261.	VII.	ELIZA ANGELINE, b. Feb. 17, 1831; m. Aug. 23, 1854, James Nelson. Residence, Buffalo, N. Y.
262.	VIII.	HELEN MAR, b. Nov. 17, 1835; m. June 29, 1857, George Washington Talcott. They reside in Buffalo, N. Y.
263.	IX.	JAMES MONROE, b. May 8, 1838; m. Dec. 5, 1865, Frances Calista Edes. Residence, Verona.

51.

Betsey Resseguie, born in Northampton, N. Y., Aug. 15, 1794; married October 1, 1816, Joel Gray, son of Edward and Sarah (Rowley) Gray, who was born in Haddam, Conn., June 24, 1790, and died July 3, 1873. Mr. Gray removed, when a small lad, to Williamstown, Mass., with his parents, and when about thirteen years old to Chenango County, N. Y., then to Verona, Oneida County, locating on the bank of Oneida Creek, where his father soon afterward died. He learned the shoemaker's trade, and, after his marriage, carried on a tanner's and currier's business also. In 1830 he purchased a farm in Westmoreland, N. Y., just across the town line from his former home, where he resided the greater remaining part of his life. He was a member of the Methodist Episcopal Church, and, for many years, chorister.

Mrs. Gray died in Rome, Aug. 13, 1886, lacking but two days of fulfilling her ninety-second year, and retained her faculties in a remarkable degree to the end. "Thus ended a life full of good deeds, unbounded charity towards all; beloved and revered by her descendants and her entire circle of acquaintances; a life and example fit for all to imitate."

CHILDREN. (*Fifth Generation.*)

264. I. GEORGE EDWARD, b. Sept. 12, 1818; m. March 29, 1843, Adaline Goodrich, who d. Dec. 6, 1845; m. (2d) Feb. 25, 1857, Lucinda Susanna Corning, b. Sept. 20, 1828; d. May 5, 1881. He resides in San Francisco, Cal.
265. II. CAROLINE, b. Jan. 17, 1820; d. Oct., 1821.
266. III. BETSEY ANN, b. Feb. 14, 1822; d. Oct. 30, 1862; m. Sept. 26, 1843, Samuel Peter Allen, b. Aug. 6, 1816; d. Sept. 9, 1870.
267. IV. ALEXANDER, b. April 29, 1824; m. March 22, 1849, Sarah Smith, who d. March 19, 1868; m. (2d) Sept. 21, 1869, Harriet Newel Ferris. They reside in Rome, N. Y.
268. V. SARA JANE, b. May 8, 1826; m. Oct. 22, 1852, Charles Corydon Howe, b. Aug. 11, 1826; d. Feb. 13, 1865. She resides in Westmoreland, N. Y.
269. VI. JOEL, b. Nov. 24, 1827; d. Nov. 20, 1861.
270. VII. CAROLINE, b. March 1, 1830; d. Sept. 8, 1843.
271. VIII. NOAH DUANE, b. Dec. 14, 1833; m. May 9, 1866, Ruth Hamilton Cole. They live in Syracuse, N. Y.

53.

Timothy Resseguie, born in Northampton, N. Y., March 15, 1798; died in Rome, March 28, 1865. He married, in 1826, Eliza Allen, daughter of Major John and Elizabeth (Wall) Allen of Oneida County. She was born in March, 1806, and died Aug. 27, 1868. Mr. Resseguie was a farmer. In 1830 he removed to Westmoreland, and took a contract for stone-work on the Erie Canal, then in process of construction, and continued in this business until 1845. In 1840 he removed to Rome, and lived there until his death. He was a man of rather taciturn disposition; of the strictest integrity and of very religious habits; making it a practice while engaged upon the public works to hold religious services amongst his men upon the Sabbath, preaching to them himself. He was a member of the Methodist communion and a trustee in the church, and while earnest in his own convictions was tolerant of other views than his own, and conceded to all men liberty of conscience.

FOURTH GENERATION.

CHILDREN. (*Fifth Generation.*)

272. I. CHARLES EDWIN, b. April 26, 1827; m. Feb. 9, 1859, Ellen Climan Hatch, b. April 22, 1827; d. March 29, 1884. He resides in Luddington, Mich.
273. II. HANNAH MARY, b. April 17, 1830; m. Jan. 18, 1851, James Tompkins Watson, b. May 2, 1830. They reside in Clinton, N. Y.
274. III. RICHARD WATSON, b. Sept. 24, 1836; d. Oct. 22, 1863; m. Nov. 20, 1859, Delia Ann Matthews, who m. (2d) April 9, 1866, Alonzo Tice of Rome, N. Y. They reside in that city.
275. IV. JOHN DEMPSTER, b. June 29, 1840; d. Dec. 11, 1865.

54.

Joel Resseguie, born in Northampton, N. Y., April 5, 1800; died in Upper Canada, Sept. 13, 1848. He married Margaret Ann Hess, daughter of John and Mary (Burns) Hess of Durhamville, N. Y. She died in November, 1877. Mr. Resseguie was a farmer.

CHILDREN. (*Fifth Generation.*)

276. I. TIMOTHY, b. May 2, 1834; m. Dec. 31, 1856, Lois Eastman. They live in Custer, Mich.
277. II. CORDELIA ANN, b. June 2, 1836; d. Jan. 13, 1878; m. Oct. 16, 1856, George Nial Eastman, b. Dec. 26, 1833.
278. III. MARGARET ANN, b. Dec. 5, 1838; m. Dec. 23, 1878, George Nial Eastman, whose first wife was her sister, Cordelia Ann. They reside in Imlay, Mich.
279. IV. JOEL DELOS, b. Jan. 14, 1842; m. Dec. 24, 1869, Mary Helen King. They reside in Saginaw City, Mich.
280. V. ELLEN ELIZA, b. Nov. 22, 1844; m. Sept. 28, 1867, William Joseph Burney, b. Dec. 12, 1843. They reside in Forest, Ontario.
281. VI. MARY ELIZABETH, b. March 22, 1847; m. Dec. 30, 1870, Robert McFarland, b. May 11, 1843. They reside in Warwick, Ont.

55.

Abigail Resseguie, born in Northampton, N. Y., Nov. 7, 1802; died in Ridgeway, Michigan, Sept. 2, 1869. She married in 1825, in Northampton, Abner Stephens, son of John Squire Stephens of Connecticut. He was born June 26, 1801, and died in Lenox, Mich., Feb. 14, 1882. Mr. Stephens removed from his birthplace to Tompkins County, N. Y., and in the fall of 1834 with his family, to Onondaga County, remaining there but two years however, when in May, 1836, he emigrated to Michigan and settled in Lenox, seven miles from the nearest white neighbor and surrounded by wild beasts and Indians. After a residence of thirty years in this town he removed to Armada in the same county, but returned to Lenox in 1875. For a number of years he filled the office of justice of the peace.

CHILDREN. (*Fifth Generation.*)

282.   I. JOEL RESSEGUIE, b. Sept. 5, 1826; d. April 12, 1871; m. Dec. 1, 1852, Clarina Jane Dryer, who d. Sept., 1866. They lived in Lenox, Mich.
283.   II. JAMES ALEXANDER, b. April 9, 1828; m. Dec. 25, 1852, Sarah Jane Wilson, who d. June 15, 1866; m. (2d) March 22, 1874, Martha Swem Ayres. They reside in Duluth, Minn.
284. III. MARY JANE, b. July 14, 1829; m. June 12, 1846, Stephen Claggett. Residence, Richmond, Mich.
285.   IV. JUSTUS, b. July 20, 1831; m. June 10, 1855, Maria Tappen. They live in Van Buren, N. Y.
286.   V. ABNER, b. July 7, 1833; d. Feb. 26, 1850.
287.   VI. CAROLINE AMANDA, b. Sept. 19, 1835; m. Jan. 29, 1852, Joshua Henry Kirkham, b. Feb. 13, 1832. They reside at High Forest, Minn.
288. VII. BETSEY MARIA, b. Feb. 5, 1839.
289. VIII. JOHN CHASE, b. Aug. 1, 1842; d. March 2, 1863.
290.   IX. CORNELIA, b. Jan. 9, 1845; d. March 11, 1871; m. Nov., 1869, John Wesley England, who d. Jan. 21, 1881. They lived at Armada, Mich.

57.

Mary Resseguie, born in Milton, N. Y., Jan. 12, 1809; died in Madison County, Sept. 30, 1840. She married Aaron Hess, a farmer, son of John Hess of Durhamville, N. Y.

CHILDREN. (*Fifth Generation.*)

291.   I. EDWIN LEE, b. Nov. 4, 1828; m. Sept. 5, 1869, Frances Carpenter. They reside in California.
292. II. JOHN.
293. III. CORDELIA.

58.

David Resseguie, born May 19, 1784; died in Northampton, N. Y., March 21, 1882. He married, March 5, 1805, Mary Case, daughter of Aaron and Patience (Simmons) Case of Northampton. She was born in Massachusetts, and died in Northville, N. Y., July 14, 1871. Mr. Resseguie removed with his parents from Connecticut to Charlton, N. Y., and from there to Northampton (then Broadalbin), reaching that place when he was three years old. He served in the war of 1812, walking from Northampton to Sackett's Harbor with his brother Charles, to enlist. He served through the war, and during the last twenty years of his life drew a government pension. He was a member of the Methodist Church and very hospitable in his entertainment of the brethren. He died at the age of 97 years and 10 months, having resided in Northampton over ninety-four years.

CHILDREN. (*Fifth Generation.*)

294. I. MIRANDA, b. Aug. 2, 1806; m. Nov. 15, 1826, Isaac Groesbeck, who d. April 11, 1840; m. (2d), Feb. 10, 1845, Joshua Wells, Jr., who d. Feb. 18, 1860. She resides in Northville, N. Y.
295. II. MARIA, b. Aug. 2, 1806; d. June 2, 1824.
296. III. JOHN, b. Feb. 8, 1808; m. Jan. 20, 1830, Velitta Palmer, who d. March 31, 1878. He resides in Northville, N. Y.
297. IV. ALEXANDER CASE, b. Sept. 13, 1809; m. Feb. 24, 1839, Jerusha Norton, b. June 10, 1816. They reside in Janesville, Wis.
298. V. RUFUS, b. Feb. 23, 1811; m. Aug. 28, 1845, Lydia Ann Bennem, who d. Dec. 17, 1851; m. (2d), June 22, 1853, Phebe Amelia Blachly. They reside in Brooklyn, N. Y.
299. VI. MARY, b. Feb. 17, 1813; m. Nov. 23, 1830, Ebenezer Gifford, b. Feb. 26, 1804. They reside in Hunter, Ill.
300. VII. HIRAM, b. June 13, 1815; m. Jan. 8, 1840, Mary M. Rogers, b. June 1, 1818. They reside in Northville, Dak.
301. VIII. HANNAH, b. July 3, 1821; m. May 17, 1842, Joseph McCuen. They live in Northville, N. Y.

59.

Mary Resseguie, born Jan. 29, 1787; died in Houndsfield, N. Y., Jan. 18, 1845. She married in 1804, Joshua Crouch, who died in Houndsfield, Feb. 6, 1873. He was a farmer. He married, for a second wife, Almira Morey, who is still living.

CHILDREN. (*Fifth Generation.*)

302. I. ESTHER, d. in infancy.
303. II. DANIEL RESSEGUIE, disappeared.
304. III. CYNTHIA, b. Feb. 9, 1811; d. May 16, 1856; m. Feb. 8, 1827, Sylvenus Tyler, b. Nov. 16, 1805. He m. (2d), Feb. 11, 1864, Maria Moore, and resides in Sackett's Harbor, N. Y.
305. IV. HANNAH FIELD, b. June 20, 1814; d. July 4, 1875; m. Dec. 31, 1834, Erasmus Darwin Maxon. He resides in Farmersville, Cal.
306. V. WILLIAM HARRISON, b. Feb. 20, 1817; m. Sept. 1, 1843, Jane Chaffee, b. Jan. 15, 1820. They reside at Sackett's Harbor, N. Y.

307. VI. SAMUEL, d. Feb. 10, 1836.
308. VII. JOHN, d. in infancy.
309. VIII. EMILY SEMANTHA, b. Jan. 15, 1828; m. May 6, 1849, Martin Puffer Lawrence, b. Dec. 4, 1825. They reside in Houndsfield, N. Y.

61.

Hannah Mariah Resseguie, born in 1790; died in Houndsfield Dec. 25, 1813. She married, in 1810, Spafford Field of Watertown, N. Y. He was born in Woodstock, Vt., April 10, 1790, and died in Houndsfield, Aug. 24, 1870. Mr. Field was brought up on a farm, and at the age of 16 removed to Field Settlement, Watertown, and in 1811 to East Houndsfield. During the war with Great Britain (1812) he was employed by the government in building the naval vessel "New Orleans" at Sackett's Harbor, and at the battle of that place served as a minute man. For his services he was granted 160 acres of government land. He was a trustee of the Christian church in East Houndsfield.

CHILD. (*Fifth Generation.*)

310. I. MARY, b. June 6, 1811; m. March 19, 1832, Nathaniel Warren Green, b. 1809. They reside at Richmond, Pa.

62.

Daniel Resseguie, born in Northampton, N. Y., March 9, 1792; died there, May 25, 1867. He married in Benson, N. Y., about 1819, Eunice Crane, daughter of Amariah and Elizabeth (Colburn) Crane of Benson. She was born Sept. 9, 1796, and died in Northampton, June 9, 1870. Mr. Resseguie was a farmer.

CHILDREN. (*Fifth Generation.*)

311. I. ORVILLE, b. Aug. 4, 1823; m. 1844, Mary Sherman, b. Sept. 16, 1829. They were divorced. m. (2d), March 15, 1857, Mary Eleanor Gilman, deceased.
312. II. MARY, b Aug. 2, 1825; m. Oct. 6, 1847, John Halpin, Jr., who d. June 12, 1857. She resides in Cleveland, Ohio.

64.

Charles Resseguie, born in Northampton, N. Y., Sept. 9, 1797; died in Edinburgh, Saratoga County, April 18, 1881. He married in Northampton, Jan. 20, 1830, Lucy Corey, daughter of Joseph and Anna (Runnells) Corey of that place. She died in

Edinburgh, Dec. 13, 1880. In 1840 Charles Resseguie removed from the old homestead of which, at that time, he was the owner, to a new and larger farm in the town of Edinburgh about three miles distant, where the remainder of his life was passed. At the beginning of the war of 1812 he walked, with his brother David, to Sackett's Harbor, where the latter enlisted; but he, being too young, was employed to draw wood to the barracks, in which occupation he continued until the close of the war. During the construction of the Erie Canal, he had the superintendence of a portion of the work, but afterward settled down to farm life. He was a deacon in the Methodist Church, and was honored and respected by all who knew him.

CHILDREN. (*Fifth Generation.*)

- 313. I. CHARLES EDWIN, b. April 3, 1833; d. March 10, 1866, m. Feb. 17, 1858, Elizabeth Brown.
- 314. II. SAMUEL PLATT, b. Sept. 7, 1834; d. Aug. 23, 1837.
- 315. III. DANIEL, b. Sept. 30, 1840; d. Feb. 6, 1847.
- 316. IV. LUCY ANN, b. Feb. 6, 1843; d. Feb. 16, 1843.
- 317. V. JAMES BIRNEY, b. Aug. 23, 1844; d. Jan. 23, 1856.

65.

Samuel Resseguie, born in Northampton, N. Y., Nov. 28, 1800; died in Houndsfield, March 24, 1853. He married, in 1822, Lydia Brown, daughter of John and Lydia (Sprague) Brown of Ballston, N. Y. She died July 8, 1882. With his newly married wife Mr. Resseguie removed to Houndsfield, making the journey with a yoke of cattle, and spending seven days on the way, their road being indicated by "blazed" trees. They settled on a farm of fifty acres, which, by industry and economy, had been increased to 220 acres at the time of his death.

CHILDREN. (*Fifth Generation.*)

- 318. I. DANIEL, b. Jan. 26, 1824; m. Jan. 1, 1863, Almeda Austin. They reside in Houndsfield, N. Y.
- 319. II. ESTHER, b. May 13, 1826; m. Jan. 1, 1846, Joel Hayden Phillips, now deceased; m. (2d), Nov. 18, 1863, Daniel Hall Lindsley. They live in Chaumont, N. Y.
- 320. III. BELDEN, b. April 15, 1828; d. Aug. 24, 1882; m. Jan. 1, 1852, Thurza Delavergne, who d. July 10, 1865; m. (2d), Jan. 1, 1866, Elvira Signor.
- 321. IV. SAMUEL, b. July 27, 1830; m. Oct. 29, 1854, Elvira Elizabeth Carpenter, b. July 17, 1834. They reside in Groton, Dak.

322. v. CORDELIA, b. July 18. 1833; m. April 22, 1858, Augustin Cook. Residence, Ellisburgh, N. Y.
323. VI. DAVID, b. Nov. 5, 1835; m. Jan. 17, 1860, Lovina Hunt. They reside in East Houndsfield, N. Y.
324. VII. MARY EMILY, b. June 12. 1838; m. July 9, 1860, Augustus Signor, of Sackett's Harbor, N. Y., b. 1835.
325. VIII. MINERVA, b. Aug. 1, 1840; m. Feb. 25, 1858, Charles L. Patrick. They live at Sackett's Harbor.
326. IX. JOHN BROWN, b. Nov. 2, 1842; m. July 4, 1875, Mary Shears. He resides at Spring Brook, Mich.

66.

Jacob Resseguie, born in Northampton, N. Y., Oct. 21, 1803; died in Chili, N. Y., Dec. 11, 1875. He married, in Edinburgh, N. Y., in 1826, Elizabeth Cole, daughter of David and Mercy (King) Cole of that town. She died in Chili, Aug. 23, 1865. He married (2d), May 10, 1870, Mrs. Lydia Gaskill of Rochester, N. Y., who died a few years later. Mr. Resseguie resided first at Northampton and then in Chili. For a number of years he was a contractor for railroads and canals.

CHILDREN. (*Fifth Generation.*)

327. I. JEROME, b. June 7, 1827; m. Jan. 11, 1851, Prudence C. Collins. They live in Livonia, N. Y.
328. II. FIDELIA, b. April 2, 1831; m. Jan. 6, 1852, Joseph Miller. They reside in Linden, Mich.
329. III. CHARLES LESTER, b. March 14, 1843; m. Nov. 17, 1865. Helen Ann Westervelt. They reside in Concord, Mich.

67.

Belden Resseguie, born in Northampton, N. Y., May 2, 1806; died in Shopiere, Rock County, Wis., Feb. 9, 1874. He married, in Northville, N. Y., Dec. 10, 1831, Polly Mariah Carpenter, daughter of Robert Nason and Betsey (Clark) Carpenter of Hope, Hamilton County. She was born in Reading, Vt., Nov. 2, 1812, and is living in Wilna, N. Y.

Belden Resseguie was employed as a foreman during the construction of the Erie Canal, and also took part in the work on the Black River Canal. In 1841 he purchased a farm in Wilna, Jefferson County, and combined with farming, the occupation of school teacher during the winter months.

CHILDREN. (*Fifth Generation.*)

330. I. ALEXANDER, b. April 6, 1833; d. June 22, 1866; m. Feb. 18, 1861, Mary Becker.
331. II. ELIZABETH, b. May 5, 1835; m. Oct. 1854, Charles Wilcox They were divorced; m. (2d), Oct. 1, 1876, John Robert Jackson. They reside in Cheyenne, Wy.
332. III. BELDEN, b. April 3, 1839; d. Aug. 23, 1839.
333. IV. STEPHEN HUBBARD WAKEMAN, b. Sept. 14, 1841; m. Nov. 12, 1864, Melvina Cole, who d. Feb. 23, 1885. He resides in Nuckolls County, Neb.
334. V. SAMUEL, b. Aug. 7, 1843; d. June 12, 1883; m. July 4, 1872 Sylvia Williamson.
335. VI. MARION, b. May 7, 1846; m. March 22, 1875, Ella Drake. They reside in Newfield, Mich.

69.

Minerva Resseguie, born in Northampton, N. Y., Feb. 9, 1809; died there, Aug. 28, 1839. She married, in Northampton, Jan. 11, 1832, Hiram Lewis, son of Joseph Lewis of Northville, who was born in that village, Jan. 22, 1804, and died Dec. 26, 1858. Mr. Lewis followed farming until 1852, when he removed to Beaver Falls, Lewis' County, and engaged in tanning until 1856; then returned to Northville and resided there until his death. He filled the office of assessor, highway commissioner, and overseer of the poor.

CHILDREN. (*Fifth Generation.*)

336. I. MARY MARIA, b. Oct. 10, 1832; m. Feb. 13, 1851, Watson Ashton, b. Sept. 27, 1825. They reside in Northampton, N. Y.
337. II. CELESTIA ANN, b. Sept. 22, 1835; m. Oct. 22, 1863, Abram Newcomb Van Arnam, b. Aug. 29, 1831. They reside at Beaver Falls, N. Y.
338. III. HANNAH MINERVA, b. May 13, 1839; m. Aug. 24, 1864, Martin Richtmyer Le Fevre, b. Feb. 19, 1837. They live at Beaver Falls.

70.

Thomas Cole, born in Norwalk, Conn., Oct. 22, 1780; died in Wilton, Conn., May, 1853. He married, about 1819, Betsey Mallory, daughter of Nathan and Molly (Cole) Mallory of Redding, Conn. She died in Jersey City, N. J., September, 1861. Mr. Cole was a resident of Wilton, and engaged in the wagon-making trade.

CHILDREN. (*Fifth Generation.*)

339.   I.   ELI, m. July 17, 1848, Emily Morgan, b. Dec. 21, 1831. They reside in Yonkers, N. Y.
340.   II. CHARLES EDWARD, b. Aug. 22, 1830; m. April 14, 1853, Anginette T. Green, who d. Dec. 13, 1860; m. (2d), April 15, 1861, Mrs. Julie Brown, who d. May or June, 1881; m. (3d), June 6, 1882, Georgiana Lounsbury. They reside in Wilton, Conn.
341.   III. ALMIRA, m. William H. Jelliff.
342.   IV. GEORGE, b. March 24, 1836; d. Sept. 3, 1868.

71.

Ira Cole, born Feb. 10, 1782; died in Franklin, Erie County, Pa., Aug. 24, 1860. He married, in Wilton, Conn., Nov. 3, 1802, Lydia Cole, daughter of Asa and Thankful (Fancher) Cole of that town. She died in Girard, Pa., March 2, 1874. Ira Cole moved from Wilton to Unadilla, Otsego County, N. Y., with his wife and three children in 1810, and located on a clearing of half an acre, and in time cleared a farm of 100 acres. In 1827 he removed to Franklin, Pa., and settled in a wilderness, going in and out by using marked trees as a guide. He cleared here a farm of 100 acres, upon which he remained until his death. He had a kind word for everyone and was greatly respected.

CHILDREN. (*Fifth Generation.*)

343.   I.   ESTHER MARY, b. Dec. 24, 1803; m. Sept. 15, 1822, Samuel Harvey Bessey, Jr., who d. March 22, 1879. She resides in Girard, Pa.
344.   II.   CHARLES, b. Sept. 2, 1805; d. Dec. 5, 1884; m. Sept. 12, 1824, Hannah Sisson, who d. Sept. 24, 1844; m. (2d), March 4, 1845, Laverna Jackson, who d. Sept. 2, 1881. He resided at Liberty, Kan.
345.   III. BETSEY, b. Oct. 17, 1807; d. Jan. 14, 1811.
346.   IV.   POLLY, b. Feb. 2, 1810; d. April 10, 1842; m. March 21, 1839, Jonathan Andrew Gibbs, b. Nov. 5, 1811. He resides in Brooklyn, N. Y.
347.   V.   ASA, b Feb. 13, 1815; d. June 13, 1845; m. Dec. 25, 1836, Catharine Crane. He lived in New York City.
348.   VI.   CURTIS, b. April 19, 1816; m. April 11, 1858, Phœbe Taylor. They reside in Franklin, Pa.
349.   VII. HARRIET, b. April 21, 1824; d. Nov. 30, 1838.

72.

Timothy Cole, born Aug. 28, 1784; died Aug. 18, 1865. He married, in South Salem, N. Y., July 4, 1810, Eliza Sterling,

FOURTH GENERATION.

daughter of Thaddeus Sterling of Wilton, Conn., who was born July 13, 1791, and died Jan. 6, 1866. Mr. Cole was a wagon-maker, and resided in the town of South East, N. Y.

CHILDREN. (*Fifth Generation.*)

350. I. EMORY, b. April 19, 1811; m. May 10, 1841, Mary Ann Sutton, (daughter of Susan Resseguie, 188), who d. June 23, 1856; m. (2d), May 9, 1860, Frances Mary Stevens, b. April 3, 1832. They reside in Pawling, N. Y.
351. II. GEORGE, b. Feb. 14, 1813; m. Dec. 31, 1840, Melissa Townsend. They reside in Southeast, N. Y.
352. III. SALLY, b. Feb. 15, 1817; d. March 17, 1864; m. April 3, 1859, Warren Barnabas Collamer, b. Feb. 2, 1823.
353. IV. MARY, b. April 8, 1818; d. March 20, 1838.
354. V. JANE, b. Feb. 21, 1819; m. Nov. 5, 1851, Charles Sherman Marsh. Residence, Rockford, Ill.
355. VI. MINERVA, b. Feb. 15, 1821; d. April 19, 1849.
356. VII. ELIZA ANN, b. Feb. 1, 1828; d. Oct. 21, 1858; m. March 17, 1857, Warren Barnabas Collamer, who subsequently married her sister Sally. He resides in Wilton, N. Y.
357. VIII. ANGELINE, b. Sept. 16, 1832. Resides at Saratoga, N. Y.
358. IX. EDWIN, b. March 20, 1836; m. Feb. 12, 1861, Clarissa Fowler. They live at Verbank, N. Y.

73.

Sally Cole, born Feb. 9, 1788; died June 28, 1863. She married, in Wilton, Conn., March 12, 1809, David Nichols, son of David and Sarah (Thomas) Nichols of Redding, who was born Sept. 28, 1786, and died Feb. 28, 1862. They resided in Wilton, next in Rhinebeck, N. Y., and lastly in Redding, Conn.

CHILDREN. (*Fifth Generation.*)

359. I. WILLIAM, b. March 23, 1811; m. Jan. 20, 1833, Polly Osborne, b. Nov. 16, 1812. They reside in Wilton, Conn.
360. II. GEORGE SHERMAN, b. March 23, 1811; d. Dec. 19, 1881; m. Jan. 20, 1837, Julia Ann Edmonds, who d. July 9, 1840; m. (2d) Feb. 25, 1844, Abby Jane Sturges, who d. Aug. 22, 1856; m. (3d) Nov. 28, 1861, Elvira Rand. He lived in Wilton, Conn.
361. III. INFANT, b. March 12, 1814; died.
362. IV. SALLY ANN, b. May 26, 1819; m. Feb. 28, 1844, James Sturges. They live in Wilton.
363. V. HARRIET, b. Aug. 14, 1821; d. April 14, 1864; m. Dec. 31, 1844, Thaddeus Smith Quick, b. Jan. 23, 1824; d. Feb. 10, 1850; m. (2d), Frederick S. Renoud, who lives at New Rochelle, N. Y.

74.

Curtis Cole, born May 10. 1790; married Mary Sturges, daughter of James and Mary (Dikeman) Sturges of Weston, Conn. He lived in Huntington, Conn.

CHILDREN. (*Fifth Generation*.)

364. I. JULIE ANN, b. March 17, 1823; m. April 9, 1848, Joseph Elnathan Fields. They reside in Easton, Conn.
365. II. JAMES STURGES, b. Sept. 19, 1825; m. April 27, 1851, Emeline Mallette, b. Sept. 29, 1831. They reside at Black Rock, Bridgeport, Conn.

75.

Samuel Cole, born in Wilton, Conn., Oct. 22, 1791; died there, April 8, 1851. He married, June 9, 1816, Deborah Eagleston, who was born in South East, N. Y., Dec. 8, 1792, and died there, Aug. 6, 1869. After their marriage they lived in Patterson, N. Y., then for about twenty years in South East, and three years before Mr. Cole's death removed to Wilton.

CHILDREN. (*Fifth Generation*.)

366. I. WILLIAM, b. Oct. 6, 1817; m. Oct. 4, 1841, Mary A. Field. They reside in Palenville, N. Y.
367. II. ALONZO, b. Oct. 3, 1819; m. Oct. 5, 1843, Mary Stevens, who d. Feb. 2, 1879, m. (2d) 1881, Maria A. Pixley.
368. III. AUGUSTUS, b. March 24, 1821; d. Nov. 7, 1828.
369. IV. HENRY, b. Jan. 21, 1823; m. Nov. 3, 1844, Mary Bailey, who d. Feb. 1862. He again married, and lives near Troy, N. Y.
370. V. MARY ELIZA, b. Oct. 17, 1824; m. Jan. 19, 1845, Daniel Forward Stevens, b. Oct. 24, 1814. They live in South East, N. Y.
371. VI. CAROLINE, b. Sept. 10, 1828; m. Dec. 27, 1845, Milton G. Lent. She resides at Brewster, N. Y.
372. VII. AUGUSTUS, b June 9, 1830; m. Mary Martin, and resides at Towners, N. Y.
373. VIII. CHARLES, b. June 7, 1834; m. 1858, Amanda A. Vandenberg.
374. IX. LUCY ANN, b. Jan. 18, 1839; m. Jan. 16, 1861, John Warren Renoud, b. March 7, 1813; d. Jan. 11, 1882; m. (2d), March 3, 1887, Egbert W. Gilbert of Danbury, Conn.

76.

Sherman Cole, born in Wilton, Conn., June 4, 1804; died in Norwalk, Conn., May 28, 1879. He married in Wilton, Dec. 10, 1829, Susan Hurlbutt, daughter of Lewis and Mollie (Scribner)

Hurlbutt of that town, who was born there Oct. 13, 1812. Mr. Cole was a hub and carriage manufacturer in Wilton. In 1854 he removed to Norwalk, and for ten years carried on the grocery business. He was one of the founders of the Zion's Hill M. E. Church in Wilton, and a member of its board of trustees; was selectman of the town, and its representative in the State Legislature. He was one of the original members of the Second M. E. Church in Norwalk, and also a trustee. "He was of a very happy disposition. To his family he was earnestly devoted, sacrificing everything for their comfort and education. When the society was being formed to erect the Second M. E. Church, he was among the first to put his shoulder under the heavy burden. He sympathized and labored and gave to the extent of his ability; when disaster came, his cheerful spirit encouraged the weaker brethren. He was a member of the first official board, and never flagged while health permitted him to bear his part of the burden of the church."

CHILDREN. (*Fifth Generation.*)

375. I. EMILY, b. Dec. 23, 1830; m. Nov. 1, 1854, Charles Van Hoosear, b. April 13, 1831; d. Dec. 1, 1881. He lived in Norwalk, Conn.

376. II. JANE, b. Aug. 18, 1832; m. Nov. 19, 1854, William Berkley Osborn. They reside in Sharon, Mich.

377. III. ELIZA, b. March 19, 1834; m. April 15, 1861, William Aaron Ambler, b. Dec. 26, 1834. They reside in Norwalk.

378. IV. IRA, b. May 4, 1836; m. Nov. 3, 1868, Rebecca Isaacs Hill, b. Oct. 3, 1847. They reside in Norwalk.

379. V. MARY ESTHER, b. Sept. 2, 1838; m. April 5, 1866, Willis McDonald. They live in Brooklyn, N. Y.

380. VI. HATTIE, b. Nov. 17, 1840; m. Aug. 1, 1870, Phineas Rice Dusinberre. They reside in Stamford, Conn.

381. VII. LYDIA ANNA, b. May 14, 1843; m. Nov. 20, 1867. Henry Stanton Selleck. They reside in Norwalk.

382. VIII. THEODORE, b. Aug. 4, 1845; d. Dec. 27, 1847.

383. IX. HENRY, b. Dec. 7, 1847; m. Dec. 8, 1873, Mary Ellen Vaille. They live in Brooklyn, N. Y.

384. X. ALLEE, b. Jan. 16, 1850; m. July 10, 1883, Elizabeth Ellen Martyn. Residence, Norwalk.

385. XI. LESTER SHERMAN, b. Dec. 24, 1852; m. Sept. 4, 1871, Sarah Eva Vaille, sister of his brother Henry's wife, b. July 20, 1852. They live in Norwalk.

386. XII. FREDERICK VICTOR, b. Jan. 18, 1855; m. Oct. 17, 1883 Kate Frances Hall. They reside in Norwalk.

78.

Ellen Resseguie, born in Ridgefield, Conn., Aug. 5, 1767; died in Geneva, N. Y., June 17, 1862. She married about 1790-1, Thomas Mead, a weaver, son of Joseph and Thankful (Rockwell) Mead. He was born about 1764, and died in Ridgefield, May, 1843. Mr. Mead served as a private in the Revolutionary War.

CHILDREN. (*Fifth Generation.*)

387. I. Harriet, b. May 30, 1793; d. March 17, 1878; m. Feb. 24, 1819, Daniel Darrin, Jr., b. Dec. 21, 1794; d. Jan. 9, 1878.
388. II. Lyman, b. 1795; d. March 31, 1859; m. Catharine Pynckney.
389. III. Cyrus, b. about 1797; d. young.
390. IV. Wakeman, b. about 1799; d. young.
391. V. Lewis, b. May 13, 1802; d. June 29, 1883; m. June 4, 1821, Sarah Lockwood, b. Nov. 24, 1802; d. Dec. 13, 1844; m. (2d), Nov. 14, 1845, Jane Murray, b. April 19, 1802; d. July 5, 1879.
392. VI. Cyrus Alanson, b. July 13, 1804; d. Sept. 7, 1882; m. Feb. 4, 1832, Jemima Clement Forbes, b. Jan. 24, 1815; d. June 13, 1878.
393. VII. Amos, b. April 13, 1808; d. March 26, 1867; m. April 25, 1850, Jemima Barber, b. March 10, 1814. She lives in Geneva, N. Y.
394. VIII. Phylinda, b. March 28, 1812; d. June 4, 1879; m. Eli S. Benedict; (2d), Sept. 2, 1848, Harmon Cole, b. Sept. 8, 1806.

80.

Isaac Resseguie, born in Ridgefield, Conn., Oct. 7, 1772; died in Hubbardton, Vt., March 11, 1864. He married in Hubbardton in 1796, Mary Dewey, daughter of Israel and Polly (Pixley) Dewey. She was born there May 16, 1771, and died there, March 13, 1866. Mr. Resseguie went from Ridgefield when he was 16 years old, to live with his mother's brother in Hubbardton. He was a farmer; deacon in the Congregational Church, and held many town offices.

CHILDREN. (*Fifth Generation.*)

395. I. Sophronia, b. Jan. 28, 1799; d. Oct. 21, 1811.
396. II. Israel Dewey, b. Dec. 20, 1800; d. Aug. 27, 1804.
397. III. Lyman, b. April 27, 1803; d. Sept. 3, 1804.
398. IV. Franklin, b. Feb. 24, 1805; d. April 27, 1817.
399. V. Horace Dewey, b. June 11, 1808; m. Feb. 24, 1848, Maryette F. Smith, b. April 15, 1828; d. Dec. 19, 1863. He resides in Brandon, Vt.

400. VI. SARAH ANN, b. Nov. 13, 1810; d. June 14, 1834; m. about 1831, Sargent Knowlton. They lived in Orwell, Vt.

82.

James Resseguie, born in Ridgefield, Conn., Jan. 12, 1775; died in Conklin, N. Y., Nov. 29, 1857. He married, Sept. 20, 1812, Jane Wilbur, daughter of Carr Wilbur of Dutchess County, N. Y. She was born Jan. 17, 1788, and died at Silver Lake, Susquehanna County, Pa., April 21, 1830. He married (2d), July 28, 1833, Polly Doty, daughter of Prince and Lovina (Thompson) Doty of Rensselaerville, N. Y. She was born in Rensselaerville, Oct. 18, 1794, and died in Bridgewater, Pa., Aug. 31, 1840. He married (3d), in Montrose, Pa., May, 1843, Mrs. Mary Miller, widow of John Miller, and daughter of James Pudney of Fishkill, N. Y. She died in Conklin, Feb. 17, 1857. Mr. Resseguie removed from his native place and settled in Susquehanna County, Pa., and passed through the inevitable hardships of a life in the wilderness. In early life he was a Presbyterian in faith, but joined the Baptist church after his removal to Pennsylvania. He was a great reader and an excellent scholar. By trade he was a weaver. In appearance he was tall, very straight, and spare, with black hair, blue eyes, and a pale complexion.

CHILDREN. (*Fifth Generation.*)

401. I. HARVEY, b. Aug. 13, 1813; d. same day.
402. II. HIRAM, b. Aug. 13, 1813; d. same day.
403. III. EMELINE, b. March 17, 1815; d. April 1, 1865; m. Jan. 1, 1840, Owen Wilbur, b. April 22, 1809. He resides in Conklin, N. Y.
404. IV. HIRAM GARDNER, b. Aug. 12, 1817; d. Aug. 28, 1842; m. Jan. 14, 1839, Sarah Thurston Crandall, b. Feb. 17, 1817. She is again married and resides in New Milford, Pa.
405. V. SARAH JANE, b. Aug. 15, 1825; d. May 29, 1871; m. April 13, 1850, Elias Wilbur, b. March 28, 1822. He resides in Conklin, N. Y.
406. VI. MARY, b. Sept. 12, 1834; m. Jan. 19, 1853, Albert Ammerman, b. Oct. 13, 1832. They reside at Little Falls, Minn.

83.

Abraham Resseguie, born in Ridgefield, Conn., Feb. 6, 1782; died in Caldwell, Wisconsin, July 24, 1856. He married in Hubbardton, Vt., in 1813, Lovina Robinson, daughter of

Isaiah and Sarah (Foot) Robinson. She was born in Hubbardton, Aug. 18, 1786, and died in Caldwell, June 20, 1858.

Abraham Resseguie removed from his native place to Hubbardton, Vt., in 1812. He continued the cultivation of a rough and rocky farm until 1835, when with several of his neighbors he started for the west on a prospecting tour, and the following year sold his farm and removed his family to Wisconsin, or the " Northwest Territory," as it was then called, where a neighbor, Joseph Caldwell, had preceded him. The journey was made by the Erie Canal, and by boat through the great lakes, and on the first of July they landed at Pike River, now Kenosha. Mr. Caldwell had built a log house, twenty feet square, about three miles from the landing, and although possessing a large family he gladly welcomed Mr. Resseguie and his family to his hospitable abode, and found room under his roof to bestow the twenty-six persons which the combined families numbered. Soon afterward Mr. Resseguie removed to the northwestern part of Racine County, and took up a claim of 320 acres on a beautiful, fertile, well-watered prairie; built a log house and removed his family thither. His neighbor, Mr. Caldwell, had already located a claim in that section, and the place was named for him as the first proprietor, "Caldwell's Prairie." In this house the family resided for eight years, and though the cost of provisions at the lake ports was exorbitant, and food poor in quality, and often difficult to procure at all, they entertained hospitably all who passed that way. In 1844, Mr. Resseguie erected a substantial frame dwelling in which the remainder of his life was passed. Without possessing brilliant qualities that distinguished him above his fellow-men, he was a man of strict integrity, loved by his family and respected by all. " Uncle Abra'm." as he was familiarly called, was regarded by all as a friend that could always be relied upon. He was a devoted christian, a member of the Congregational Church, and always gave liberally of his means in support of the gospel.

CHILDREN. (*Fifth Generation.*)

407. I. SOPHRONIA, b. April 27, 1815; m. Feb. 4, 1834, William Alonzo Cheney, b. Dec. 31, 1806. They reside at Springvale, Wis.

408. II. BETSEY, b. April 30, 1816; m. Feb. 15, 1835, Calvin Gault, b. 1814. She resides in Caldwell, Wis.

409. III. SARAH, b. Jan. 29, 1818; d. April 23, 1861; m. Nov. 20, 1858, Sewall Andrews, b. Feb. 5, 1807; d. March 19, 1887.

410. IV. JANE, b. June 7, 1819; m. July 16, 1837, Oliver Van Valin, b. Jan. 5, 1809. They reside in Caldwell, Wis.
411. V. JAMES, b. Jan. 3, 1823; d. Sept. 2, 1864; m. Feb. 18, 1847, Angeline Walker, b. Sept. 5, 1823; d. Oct. 8, 1855; m. (2d) Oct. 12, 1856, Ellen Maria Winchell, b. April 4, 1838, who m. in 1880, A. D. Hendrickson, and resides in Waukesha, Wis.
412. VI. MARY, b. April 8, 1824; d. July 12, 1844.
413. VII. LOVINA, b. June 4, 1826; m. Oct. 31, 1848, William Scureman Cooper, b. Feb. 4, 1828; d. Sept. 2, 1862; m. (2d) Sept. 26, 1867, Oliver Houghton Sheldon, b. May 6, 1830. They reside in Grant Township, Neb.
414. VIII. ADDISON, b. Jan. 14, 1829. Resides at Aurora, Ill. Unmarried.

84.

Polly Resseguie, born in Ridgefield, Conn., Feb. 21, 1785; died in Eddytown, Yates County, N. Y., March 27, 1859. She married, in Ridgefield, Jan. 14, 1808, William Palmer, son of Thomas and Jemima (Vandeusen) Palmer of Greene County, N. Y. He was born Aug. 15, 1786, and died in Eddytown, Feb. 15, 1856. The greater part of their lives was passed in Hillsdale, Columbia County, N. Y., but in 1854 Mr. Palmer sold his farm there and removed to Eddytown.

CHILDREN. (*Fifth Generation.*)

415. I. SALLY ANN, b. March 27, 1809; d. June 13, 1854.
416. II. LEWIS RESSEGUIE, b. Aug. 29, 1810; d. Sept., 1887; m. Dec. 6, 1837, Lydia Bushnell, b. Oct. 30, 1814. She resides in Minneapolis, Minn.
417. III. JOHN, b. July 1, 1812; d. Nov. 8, 1884; m. Feb. 25, 1836, Miranda Barnes, who d. about 1842; m. (2d) Jan. 19, 1846, Amanda Kane, b. 1831. She resides at Himrods, N. Y.
418. IV. NELLY, b. Sept. 8, 1814; d. Sept. 22, 1872; m. Oct. 16, 1834, Hiram Sanford Brown, b. July 22, 1811; d. May 25, 1854.
419. V. PHEBE, b. Oct. 23, 1816; d. June 30, 1838; m. Nov. 9, 1836, Isaac Persons, Jr., b. May 6, 1810; d. July 31, 1856. They lived in Hillsdale, N. Y.
420. VI. LYMAN, b. Aug. 19, 1818; m. Sept. 9, 1846, Elizabeth Tallmadge, b. Sept. 8, 1814. They reside in Minneapolis, Minn.
421. VII. HARRIET, b. July 25, 1820; d. Dec. 1, 1877; m. Sept. 3, 1842, Francis G. Denio, b. March 31, 1814; d. July 20, 1882.
422. VIII. EMELINE AMELIA, b. Sept. 28, 1822; m. June 1, 1854, Isaac Lanning, b. July 4, 1793; d. May 24, 1879. She resides at Eddytown, N. Y.
423. IX. AUGUSTA LORINDA, b. March 12, 1825; d. Jan. 2, 1883; m. Jan. 14, 1846, Rev. Albert Rutson Knox, b. April 24, 1824. He resides at Waukegan, Ill.

424.	x.	MARY, b. June 11, 1827; d. July 21, 1874; m. May 3, 1856, Joseph E. Hicks, b. Sept. 14, 1825, who m. (2d) July 21, 1882, Jane Covert. They reside at Huston, Dak.
425.	xi.	WILLIAM, b. March 20, 1829; d. Feb. 15, 1856.

89.

William David Resseguie, born in Ridgefield, Conn., Aug. 6, 1792; died at Sing Sing, N. Y., Feb. 13, 1839. He married, May 2, 1815, Mary Forster, daughter of John Forster of Pleasantville, N. Y., where she was born March 10, 1793. She died March 23, 1839. Mr. Resseguie resided in New York city, where he pursued the trade of an upholsterer, but afterwards removed to Sing Sing.

CHILDREN. (*Fifth Generation.*)

426.	I.	WILLIAM FORSTER, b. March 30, 1816; d. Jan., 1857; m. Dec. 31, 1841, Louisa Arcularius, b. Feb. 13, 1823. She resides in Brooklyn, N. Y.
427.	II.	ALFRED, b. Sept. 10, 1817; d. Jan. 7, 1839.
428.	III.	JOHN STEPHENS, b. March 5, 1819.
429.	IV.	MARY DEAN, b. Sept. 18, 1820; d. April 22, 1821.
430.	V.	OSCAR, b. Feb. 1, 1822; m. Feb. 11, 1846, Mary Hitchcock. They reside in Sing Sing, N. Y.
431.	VI.	ISAAC TELLER, b. July 5, 1824; d. May 21, 1827.
432.	VII.	SMITH, b. Feb. 3, 1826; d. Sept. 21, 1826.
433.	VIII.	SARAH JANE, b. April 14, 1828; d. Dec. 25, 1863; m. Nov. 1852, Andrew J. Darby.
434.	IX.	ALVIRA ANTOINETTE, b. Sept. 14, 1831; d. Aug. 11, 1837.
435.	X.	MARY ELIZA, b. Aug. 15, 1832; m. Oct. 9, 1850, Alonzo Burrhus, b. Jan. 26, 1825; d. March 19, 1869. She resides in Sing Sing, N. Y.
436.	XI.	GEORGE MORTIMER, b. Aug. 3, 1836; d. Jan. 13, 1837.

92.

Samuel Resseguie, born in 1800; died in San Francisco, Cal., Jan. 26, 1855. He married Anna ———, who died in San Francisco, March 10, 1880. Mr. Resseguie left Ridgefield, Conn., his native place, and settled first in Susquehanna County, Pa., and afterward in Kenosha, Wis. From the History of Kenosha County, the following extract is taken: "On the 7th of July, 1835, Mr. Samuel Resseguie arrived in Kenosha, and, to use a squatter's phrase, "jumped the island." Mr. Resseguie brought with him a Mr. John Noble and a number of brothers by the name of Woodbridge, and others, and he accordingly had quite a formidable force to sustain him in holding possession. This circumstance occasioned the first dispute about the right of property that had occurred at this place: but the dispute, which at one time threatened to cause some disturbance, was finally amicably settled, and Mr. Resseguie retained a portion of the island, either by purchase or some other compromise. After camping on the island for about two weeks, Mr. Resseguie commenced the erection of a log house, and shortly after completing it opened it as a tavern. Although this humble public house was not equal to the Grant House, it served its purpose well. But few men knew how to cater to the appetites of their guests better than Resseguie: his table was provisioned with the best wild game the surrounding country could furnish, and the economy with which he was accustomed to stow away his numerous guests in a given area in his little garret was truly astonishing. His success was so unexpectedly great in the line of tavern-keeping that he concluded to enlarge his business; accordingly, in the following month, he opened a store in an adjoining cabin, under the firm name of Resseguie & Noble."

He subsequently emigrated to California, settled in San Francisco, and at the time of his death owned the premises known as No. 4 Wetmore Place. By his will his property was divided equally between his wife and his daughter, Eleanor Edwards. Mrs. Resseguie died at the house in Wetmore Place, leaving a will, by which her house and furniture was devised to her granddaughter, Mrs. Anna R. Smith, of Glen Rock, Nevada, and the residue of the estate to Mrs. Smith's daughter, Eleanor Galvin.

CHILD. (*Fifth Generation.*)

437.   I.   ELEANOR, b. about 1825; d. July 24, 1862; m. —— Edwards.

93.

Joel Nichols, born Nov. 11, 1774; died in Paris, Ind. He married about 1794, Sara Hubbell, daughter of Peter and Sara (Stewart) Hubbell of Wilton, Conn. She died in Rensselaerville, N. Y., Jan. 24, 1807. He married (2d) June 20, 1807, Julia Jennings, daughter of Richard and Jemima (Vail) Jennings, of Orange County, N. Y. She was born May 12, 1783, and died in Orange County, Nov. 23, 1826. He married (3d) Mrs. Polly

Humphrey. Mr. Nichols resided in Rensselaerville until about 1810, when he removed to Florida, Orange County. After his third marriage he removed to Indiana. He was a farmer.

CHILDREN. (*Fifth Generation.*)

438. I. JESSE, b. Dec. 22, 1796; lost at sea on a voyage begun in December, 1819; m. June 16, 1814, Mary White, b. June 6, 1795; d. Sept. 1850.
439. II. LUMAN, b. Jan. 1, 1798; d. Feb. 3, 1883; m. May 30, 1819, Clara Sheldon, who d. March 8, 1851. They lived at Rensselaerville, N. Y.
440. III. BETSEY HUBBELL, b. March 25, 1800; d. Sept. 15, 1884; m. Sept. 6, 1818, Jacob Hess, b. June 5, 1795; d. Jan. 26, 1878.
441. IV. MARIA JENNINGS, b. Jan. 25, 1808; m. Aug. 31, 1826, Jehiel Chilson, b. Oct. 27, 1804; d. Nov. 11, 1839; m. (2d) Aug. 3, 1841, John Morrison, b. June 10, 1806; m. (3) June 21, 1846, Asa Hurd, b. Oct. 15, 1794; d. Nov. 19, 1874. She resides in Peterborough, N. Y.
442. V. WILLIAM THORNTON, b. March 15, 1811; d. May 15, 1812.

95.

Sally Nichols, born Aug. 9, 1782; died June 27, 1865. She married, in 1798, Asa Phelps, son of Asa Phelps of Rensselaerville. He died July 24, 1840. They lived at Candor, Tioga County, N. Y.

CHILDREN. (*Fifth Generation.*)

443. I. ELECTA, b. Sept. 24, 1799; m. Martin Hendrick.
444. II. SALLY, b. March 4, 1801; m. Feb. 1, 1827, Matthew Felter, b. Jan. 11, 1806, d. Sept. 15, 1872. She resides in Richmondville, N. Y.
445. III. LUCINDA, b. Dec. 4, 1802; m. May 9, 1824, Rufus Brown, who d. Dec. 25, 1837; m. (2d) March 13, 1845, Caleb Hubbard, who d. April 6, 1861. She resides (1884) in Candor, N. Y.
446. IV. BRADFORD, b. Sept. 23, 1804; d. June 12, 1883; m. Mary Beecher, who d. Sept. 21, 1865.
447. V. HIRAM, b. May 12, 1806; d. Nov. 19, 1875; m. 1828, Martha Lennon, who d. July 25, 1834; m. (2d) March 5, 1845, Harriet Herrick, who d. April 26, 1854.
448. VI. JASON, b. July 19, 1808; d. April 19, 1884; m. Nov. 26, 1835, Clarinda Beecher, who d. Oct. 17, 1867; m. (2d) Sept. 7, 1868, Rhoda Clinton, who d. March 19, 1875; m. (3d) Nov. 25, 1875, Fannie D. Wilkson, who d. Dec. 18, 1882; m. (4th) April 18, 1883, Diana Tibbles.
449. VII. HARRIET, b. Feb. 3, 1811; m. Matthew Ayres.

FOURTH GENERATION. 67

450. VIII. JOEL, b. Jan. 23, 1813; d. April 18, 1844; m. Sept. 5, 1838, Harriet Darling, who m. (2d) Daniel Vosburgh, and resides in Candor, N. Y.
451. IX. ASA, b. Dec. 16, 1814; m. Feb. 18, 1842, Lois Amanda Beecher, sister of his brother Bradford's wife. They reside in Flemingville, N. Y.
452. X. JESSE, b. June 7, 1817; m. June 3, 1847, Minerva Hopkins Herrick. They reside in Flemingville.
453. XI. ABIGAIL MELISSA, b. July 25, 1819; m. Joseph Grimes. They reside in Colesburgh, Iowa.
454. XII. OTHNIEL, b. Nov. 6, 1821; m. March 3, 1846, Sara Abigail Grimes, who d. March 11, 1865; m. (2d) Aug. 13, 1866, Mary Jane Jacobs. They reside in Susquehanna, Pa.
455. XIII. AMANZO, b. May 11, 1824; d. Feb. 20, 1852, unmarried.
456. XIV. RHODA SELINA, b. Nov. 14, 1826; m. James Cole. They reside in Colesburgh, Iowa.

96.

Polly Smith, born in Ridgefield, Conn., Sept. 27, 1778; died there Jan. 1, 1839. She married, in Ridgefield, May 8, 1803, Benjamin Benedict, son of Jesse and Mehitable (Northrop) Benedict, who was born Jan. 17, 1770, and died July 13, 1847. He was a farmer and resided in Ridgefield.

CHILDREN. (*Fifth Generation.*)

457. I. EMILY, b. July 27, 1804; d. May 1, 1841; m. Oct. 19, 1824, Thomas Northrop, b. Dec. 8, 1805; d. April 23, 1884. They lived at Lysander, N. Y.
458. II. EDWARD, b. Oct. 26, 1805; m. Dec. 23, 1830, Maria Hoyt, who d. April 22, 1871. He resides in Butler, N. Y.
459. III. EDWIN, b. Oct. 26, 1805; d. June 1, 1876; m. Oct. 13, 1833, Catharine Nash, who d. Sept. 14, 1882. They lived in Ridgefield, Conn.
460. IV. JANE ANN, b. April 21, 1809; d. April 5, 1880; m. Oct. 14, 1832, John Harvey Benedict, b. Feb. 23, 1808; d. May 11, 1871. They lived in Ridgefield.
461. V. MARY, b. May 27, 1813; d. April 15, 1827.
462. VI. BENJAMIN SMITH, b. Jan. 27, 1817; d. Sept. 11, 1865; m. 1844, Mary Davis. She resides at Huntley, Ill.

98.

Anna Smith, born in Ridgefield, Conn., Aug. 1, 1783. She married Jeremiah Dauchey, and lived in Troy, N. Y.

CHILDREN. (*Fifth Generation.*)

463. I. SAMUEL S., married and died.
464. II. JANE, d. about 18 years old.

99.

Sally Smith, born in Ridgefield, Conn., April 5, 1786; died Oct. 31, 1880. She married, Sept. 28, 1821, Thaddeus Jewett. of Galway, Saratoga County, N. Y., who was born in the "District of Maine," probably in South Berwick, about 1784, and died May 22, 1854. His father was Dr. Nathan Jewett, who removed to Saratoga County when Thaddeus was young.

CHILDREN. (*Fifth Generation.*)

465. I. MARY, b. Sept. 25, 1822; d. Sept. 15, 1884; m. Sept. 6, 1843, William Rockwell Hoyt, who d. Aug. 24, 1875. They lived in Ridgefield.
466. II. ELIZABETH, b. Nov. 17, 1824; m. April 26, 1849, Rev. George Justus Harrison. They reside at Milton, Conn.

100.

Nathan Smith, born in Ridgefield, Conn., Nov. 11, 1788; died Feb. 20, 1856. He married Nov. 15, 1825, Sarah Stebbins Bradley, who died June 14, 1883. Mr. Smith filled the office of town clerk of Ridgefield for a number of years.

CHILDREN. (*Fifth Generation.*)

467. I. JULIA ELIZABETH, b. Feb. 27, 1830; d. Nov. 24, 1872.
468. II. NATHAN, b. Sept. 3, 1847; d. May 5, 1870.

101.

Hannah Peck, born in Danbury, Conn., Aug. 15, 1776; died in Greenfield, Ohio, March 27, 1855. She married in Danbury, Aug. 15, 1797, Eli Gregory, son of Nathan and Thankful (Benedict) Gregory of that town. He was born there Oct. 11, 1772, and died in Greenfield Sept. 18, 1841. He was a clothier and carder of wool. The family removed to Greenfield about 1825.

CHILDREN. (*Fifth Generation.*)

469. I. ALANSON PECK, b. Jan. 18, 1799; d. Aug. 18, 1839; m. Nov. 6, 1822, Huldah Vail, b. July 18, 1791; d. May 2, 1871. They lived at Greenfield, Ohio.
470. II. NATHAN BENEDICT, b. Oct. 30, 1800; d. March 18, 1818.
471. III. JOHN ALEXANDER, b. Nov. 22, 1804; m. Nov. 13, 1825, Elizabeth Osborn, b. Aug. 16, 1802; d. June 26, 1871. He lived (1885) in Crestline, Ohio.

FOURTH GENERATION.

103.

Rebeckah Peck, born in Danbury. Conn., March 20, 1783; died there Aug. 14, 1853. She married in Danbury, March 17, 1805, Eli Mygatt, son of Eli and Phebe (Judson) Mygatt of that town, where he was born March 23, 1770, and died Aug. 22, 1845.

"Eli Mygatt was a descendant in the seventh generation of Joseph Mygatt, one of the first settlers of Hartford. He was made a freeman Sept. 16, 1799. The following obituary notice is from the Danbury *Recorder:* 'But few are laid in the last resting-place of the body of a more peaceable life or possessed of a more practical philanthropy. Of an unaffected familiar manner and unchanging good humor, his cheerful countenance, welcome salutation, and kind inquiries rendered his society pleasant and imparted a good and salutary influence in his intercourse with others. He was one of that venerable class of men whose peculiar simplicity of manners and honesty of purpose are rare characteristics, and are needed as healthy examples to counteract the selfishness and insincerity which harm the characters of young men now coming upon the stage of life. He was for thirty years a member of the Congregational Church in this village.'"— *Mygatt Genealogy.*

CHILDREN. (*Fifth Generation.*)

472.	I.	WILLIAM JUDSON, b. Jan. 19, 1806; d. Sept. 4, 1869.
473.	II.	JOHN ELI, b. Aug. 27, 1807; d. July 1, 1809.
474.	III.	ELI, b. June 11, 1809; m. Oct. 24, 1837, Sophia Northrop, b. April 29, 1814. They reside in New Milford, Conn.
475.	IV.	JANE ANN, b. March 4, 1811 ; d. July 19, 1885.
476.	V.	JOHN PECK, b. Feb. 2, 1813; d. July 26, 1818.
477.	VI.	COMFORT STARR, b. Jan. 17, 1815; d. Jan. 25, 1860.
478.	VII.	HENRY THOMAS, b. Jan. 25, 1817; m. Aug. 7, 1850, Julia Losee. He resided (1885) in Danbury, Conn.
479.	VIII.	GEORGE, b. Aug. 3, 1820; m. July 22, 1845, Ellen Paris Rice, b. June 22, 1825. They reside in Brooklyn, N. Y.
480.	IX.	HARRIET AUGUSTA, b. Dec. 16, 1823; m. Dec. 5, 1885, Dr. Alfred Patten Monson, b. June 20, 1823. They reside at Daytona, Fla.

104.

John Morris Peck, born in Danbury, Conn., Oct. 7, 1786; died in Cincinnati, Ohio, Feb. 19, 1867. He married in 1811, at Salem, Mass., Rebecca Silsbee, daughter of Samuel and Rebecca (Reed) Silsbee of Salem. She was born March 9, 1791, and died in Cincinnati May 10, 1862. Mr. Peck was a hatter, and carried on that business in Salem. In 1814 he removed to Boston and kept a store on Ann street for a time; but, his business increasing, he removed to the corner of Washington street and Cornhill, having in another location a small factory for making beaver and wool hats. In 1824 he built a large brick factory in Medford, Mass., for making and finishing hats and bonnets, and also carried on an extensive fur business. In 1832 he retired from business, and in 1837 removed to Cincinnati, where his remaining years were passed.

CHILDREN. (*Fifth Generation.*)

481. I. JOHN MORRIS, b. Feb. 10, 1812; m. April 9, 1839, Elizabeth Sinnickson Fithian, b. Aug. 23, 1821; d. March 31, 1868. He lives at Red Bank, Ohio.
482. II. THOMAS RESSEGUIE, b. March 11, 1813; d. Sept. 13, 1813.
483. III. MARY SILSBEE, b. Aug. 7, 1814. Resides in Cincinnati, Ohio.
484. IV. THOMAS RESSEGUIE, b. April 13, 1816; d. Sept. 26, 1821.
485. V. REBECCA ANN, b. Aug. 8, 1817; d. Sept. 29, 1829.
486. VI. SON, unnamed, died in infancy.
487. VII. SARAH MARIA, b. June 2, 1820. Resides in Cincinnati.
488. VIII. EMILY PRINCE, b. Nov. 17, 1821; d. Sept. 7, 1867; m. May 4, 1847, Nathaniel Robinson Stout, b. June 5, 1822. He has again married, and lives at Stapleton, Staten Island, N. Y.
489. IX. EDWARD AUGUSTUS, b. May 25, 1823; m. Dec. 28, 1847, Margaret Susan Bowling, b. April 27, 1824. They reside at Anthony, Kan.
490. X. ALEXANDER GREGORY, b. Nov. 12, 1824; m. Sept. 12, 1848, Sarah McKee, b. April 25, 1825; d. Feb. 28, 1871. He resides in Cincinnati.
491. XI. ADELINE AUGUSTA, b. Jan. 12, 1827; d. Nov. 5, 1884; m. Oct. 23, 1849, Benjamin Rich Wilson, b. Feb. 21, 1826; d. Feb. 2, 1879.
492. XII. ANGELINE AMANDA, b. Sept. 6, 1828; m. Sept. 14, 1847, Edward Jonathan Wilson, brother of her sister Adeline's husband, who d. Nov. 12, 1872. She resides at Mt. Auburn, Cincinnati.
493. XIII. SON, unnamed, b. June 3, 1833; d. in infancy.

105.

Thomas Resseguie Peck, born in Danbury, Conn., April 3, 1792; died in Medford, Mass., March 8, 1882. He married in Salem, June 10, 1821, Sarah Silsbee, sister of his brother John's wife. She was born in Salem, Dec. 6, 1802, and died in Medford, Oct. 11, 1839. He married (2d) Sept. 29, 1842, in Medford, Elizabeth Bradbury, daughter of William and Elizabeth (Floyd) Bradbury of that town. She was born Aug. 14, 1792, and died Sept. 10, 1882. Mr. Peck was a hat manufacturer, and associated in business with his brother John.

FOURTH GENERATION.

CHILDREN. (*Fifth Generation.*)

494.   I. HANNAH GREGORY, b. April 18, 1822; d. Oct. 14, 1854; m. April 2, 1854, Dr. Albert Franklin Sawyer, b. Aug. 9, 1827. He resides in San Francisco, Cal.
495.   II. HARRIET RESSEGUIE, b. June 5, 1823; m. Dec. 9, 1840, Samuel Thompson Thompson, b. July 15, 1815. They reside in Ancora, N. J.
496.   III. SARAH REBECCA, b. Sept. 21, 1826; m. April 15, 1857, David Gardner Ranney, b. Feb. 2, 1816; d. Jan. 29, 1882. She resides in Boston, Mass.
497.   IV. MARY ELIZABETH, b. Sept. 21, 1826; m. Aug. 12, 1862, James Aigin Hervey, b. March 29, 1827. They reside in Medford, Mass.
498.   V. LUCY AMELIA, b. June 24, 1828; resides in Medford.
499.   VI. MARGARET SAGE, b. Nov. 29, 1830; d. Dec. 22, 1881.
500.   VII. THOMAS RESSEGUIE, b. Oct. 16, 1832; d. May 13, 1855.
501.   VIII. CAROLINE AUGUSTA, b. June 3, 1836; d. April 15, 1837.
502.   IX. JULIA ANN, b. June 3, 1836; d. March 31, 1837.
503.   X. JULIA AUGUSTA, b. April 22, 1838; m. Sept. 16, 1856, Captain Samuel Kidder Leach, b. July 10, 1819; d. Aug. 27, 1874. She resides in Boston.
504.   XI. FREDERIC SILSBEE, b. Sept. 20, 1839; d. May 8, 1841.

106.

William Prime, born in New Milford, Conn., June 7, 1779; died in Poughkeepsie, N. Y., Aug. 1, 1828. He married in New Milford, Anna Canfield, daughter of Isaac and Hannah (Lamson) Canfield, who was born March 28, 1779, and died in South Britain, Conn., March 27, 1851.

CHILDREN. (*Fifth Generation.*)

505.   I. PHEBE MARIA, b. Feb. 8, 1819; d. Feb. 25, 1858; m. Jan. 25, 1843, Benjamin Philo Downes, b. Feb. 2, 1807; d. Nov. 6, 1862.
506.   II. WILLIAM ISAAC, b. Sept. 11, 1822; d. Feb. 22, 1843.

107.

Phebe Prime, born in New Milford, Conn., May 4, 1781; died there Nov. 11, 1862. She married, April 11, 1804, in New Milford, Abel Canfield, Jr., son of Abel and Rebecca (Beardslee) Canfield. He died in that town, May 27, 1869, aged 90 years. He was a farmer.

CHILDREN. (*Fifth Generation.*)

507. I. WILLIAM NELSON, b. March 13, 1805; m. April 8, 1835, Martha Ann Platt, b. May 19, 1809; d. June 7, 1872; m. (2d) Oct. 15, 1875, Mrs. Ruth Garnet (Denio) Fuller, b. July 13, 1823. They reside at New Milford, Conn.
508. II. ALANSON NORMAN, b. Oct. 6, 1807; m. March 29, 1837, Mercy Lines, b. June 20, 1806. They reside at New Milford.
509. III. JANE ANN, b. July 1, 1809; d. March 4, 1885.
510. IV. RALPH EDWIN, b. Dec. 1, 1812. Resides at New Milford, unmarried.
511. V. REBECCA SOPHIA, b. April 11, 1823; m. Oct. 18, 1866, Merritt Beach, b. July 29, 1817. They reside at New Milford.

108.

Jane Prime, born in New Milford, Conn., Nov. 11, 1782; died there April 14, 1864. She married in that town, Dec. 23, 1810, Samuel Treadwell, son of Hezekiah and Abiah (Stilson) Treadwell. He was born there May 5, 1788, and died June 1, 1867.

CHILDREN. (*Fifth Generation.*)

512. I. JOHN PRIME, b. Oct. 6, 1811; d. April 8, 1876; m. Dec. 8, 1841, Mary Esther Lockwood, b. Sept. 25, 1815; d. March 17, 1880. They lived in New York city.
513. II. HENRY RESSEGUIE, b. Jan. 17, 1817; m. May 16, 1843, Martha Downs Mygatt, b. Feb. 13, 1823; d. May 21, 1859; m. (2d) April 3, 1879, Clarissa Ruth Mygatt, sister of his first wife, b. Sept. 9, 1832. They live in New Milford.
514. III. PHEBE LUCRETIA, b. Dec. 4, 1821; m. Feb. 4, 1852, Alexander Marshall Anderson, b. Feb. 2, 1804; d. Jan. 5, 1877. She resides in New Milford.

109.

Asa Prime, born in New Milford, Conn., Nov. 16, 1791; died in Croton, Delaware County, N. Y., March 21, 1829. He married, April 16, 1815, in New Milford, Abiah Hull Treadwell, daughter of Hezekiah and Esther (Hull) Treadwell. She was born in New Milford, April 10, 1797, and is now living (1886) in Pennsylvania. Mr. Prime was a man of feeble health; he followed the occupations of merchant, teacher, farmer, and hotel keeper, the latter at Croton, whither he removed in 1825 from New Milford.

FOURTH GENERATION.

CHILDREN. (*Fifth Generation.*)

515.   I.   ROYAL TREADWELL, b. Oct. 6, 1819; m. June 11, 1873, Harriet Smith Houghtaling, b. March 4, 1847. They reside at Croton, N. Y.

516.   II. ESTHER CORDELIA, b. April 2, 1824; m. Feb. 12, 1845, George Hotchkiss, b. March 21, 1818; d. July 25, 1874; m. (2d) Nov. 29, 1882, John Beardslee, b. June 12, 1812. They reside at Little Meadows, Pa.

517.   III. ALMON HEZEKIAH, b. Sept. 15, 1826; d. Sept. 30, 1870; m. March 14, 1861, Josephine E. Merrell. He lived at Oxford, N. Y.

110.

Samuel Nichols, born in Connecticut, Oct. 5, 1779; died in Fenner, N. Y. (Mile-Strip), Jan. 19, 1871. He married in Rensselaerville, N. Y., Oct. 23, 1800, Catharine Hess, daughter of Deidrick and Maria (Tinklepaugh) Hess of that place. She died in Fenner, Jan. 6, 1869. Mr. Nichols removed to Fenner in 1802, with his father, and settled on the Mile-Strip,* where they cleared a farm. He was a Methodist; a trustee in the Society; held several town offices and was a justice of the peace. He served at the front for a short time, during the war of 1812, and had command of a company.

CHILDREN. (*Fifth Generation.*)

518.   I.   RUFUS HESS, b. Oct. 30, 1803; m. Nov. 11, 1827, Tacy Culver, who d. April 2, 1850; m. (2d) Aug. 17, 1851, Prudence B. Lamb. They reside in Fenner, N. Y.

519.   II. CATHARINE MARIA, b. July 3, 1825; m. Oct. 3, 1865, Samuel Frisbie. They reside in Mile-Strip, N. Y.

111.

Lucinda Nichols, born June 24, 1781; died in Coldwater, Mich., Jan 13, 1862. She married Moses Rice, a shoemaker and tanner, who served as a soldier in the war of 1812, and died

---

* "From a part of the new Petersburgh tract and also the Mile-Strip, the town of Fenner was formed. The former was leased of the Indians in 1794, and purchased in 1797; the latter was granted by the Oneidas from their reservation to the State, and was called the 'Cowaselon tract'; it contained twenty-five lots, and lay between the Cowaselon and Chittenango Creeks, and from the fact of its being a mile across it was named 'Mile-Strip', this title having passed into all legal documents pertaining thereto."—*History of Madison County, N. Y.*

from the effects of wounds at or near Buffalo, N. Y. His residence was in the Mile-Strip, Fenner, but at the time of his death his family were living in the town of Lenox.

CHILDREN. (*Fifth Generation.*)

520. I. BILLINGS ROBINSON, b. May 15, 1802; d. May 7, 1880; m. 1820, Laura Lucinda Brownson, who d. May 23, 1869. They lived in Fenner, N. Y.
521. II. HARRY NICHOLS, b. Oct. 28, 1804; m. Dec. 31, 1827, Eede Ellen Strong, who d. June 8, 1876. He lived (1884) in Spencer, O.
522. III. HORATIO, b. 1806; d. at 9 years of age.
523. IV. WARREN MOSES, b. March 8, 1811; d. Nov., 1881; m. Oct., 1838, Amanda M. Noble, who d. Aug. 18, 1877.
524. V. MARIA HANNAH, b. May 13, 1813; d. July 27, 1876; m. 1837, Dr. Alonzo D. Blye, who d. July 29, 1876. They lived in Coldwater, Mich.

112.

Annis Nichols, born Oct. 18, 1783; died Dec. 12, 1812. She married Peter Love, who deserted her and went to parts unknown. She returned to her father's house, where she passed her life.

CHILD. (*Fifth Generation.*)

525. I. ZEPHANIAH, d. in childhood.

113.

Hannah Nichols, born Aug. 14, 1785; died Aug. 7, 1868. She married, Aug. 30, 1804, Jacob Bump, who was born Sept. 8, 1779, and died Nov. 24, 1848. They resided in Fenner, N. Y.

CHILDREN. (*Fifth Generation.*)

526. I. MARY, b. Sept. 16, 1805; m. March 16, 1828, John Pray, b. Oct. 3, 1806; d. Aug. 5, 1865. She resides at Mount Morris, N. Y.
527. II. ANNIS, b. March 25, 1808; d. Feb. 28, 1885; m. Jan. 6, 1831, John Fort, Jr., b. Sept. 29, 1805; d. Jan. 20, 1876. They lived in Lowell, Mich.
528. III. HARVEY RESSEGUIE NICHOLS, b. April 4, 1816; d. May 30, 1882; m. 1851, Catharine Rossier, b. 1827. She resides in Brighton, N. Y.

116.

Harry Nichols, born Feb. 1, 1789; died in Penfield, Mich., March 18, 1846. He married Rhoda Smith, who died in Mar-

FOURTH GENERATION.

shall, Mich., March 17, 1874. Mr. Nichols removed to Michigan in 1837, first settling at Grass Lake, where he remained a year, and from there removed to Penfield. He was a farmer. After his death the widow sold the farm and removed to Marshall, where she lived with her daughter, Lucinda, until her death.

CHILDREN. (*Fifth Generation.*)

529. I.   SAMUEL, b. about 1812; d. about 10 years of age.
530. II. MATILDA, b. about 1814; m. about 1832, Trumbull Denton, and d. soon after.
531. III. MELISSA, b. about 1816; m. about 1836, Alonzo Allen, and d. six or eight years after. They lived in Schroeppel, N. Y.
532. IV. LUCINDA JANE, b. about 1820; d. March 29, 1882; m. 1841, George W. Knox, b. 1815; d. March, 1856; m. (2d) 1859, Jacob. T. Root, who d. Sept., 1884. They lived in Marshall, Mich.
533. V.   MORILDA, b. about 1822; d. about 1849; m. about 1844, William Shannon, who d. in 1869.
534. VI. HELEN MAR, b. 1827; d. Feb. 14, 1858; m. Aug. 17, 1848, Amos Van Valin, who d. Feb. 2, 1885. They lived in Marshall, Mich.

118.

William Nichols, born May 14, 1795; died July 6, 1881. He married at Sullivan, Madison County, N. Y., Sept. 19, 1813, Nancy Randall, daughter of David and Subrina (Ferry) Randall. She died in Peterborough, N. Y., March 1, 1825. He married (2d) in Fenner, N. Y., Sept. 26, 1826, Huldah Kelsey, daughter of Reuben and Grace (Weed) Kelsey. She died in Perryville, N. Y. He married (3d) in Perryville, Catharine Storms. Mr. Nichols was a shoemaker.

CHILDREN. (*Fifth Generation.*)

535. I.   HANNAH SUBRINA, b. Aug. 14, 1814; m. Feb. 10, 1833, Benjamin Smith Durkee, b. Feb. 9, 1812; d. May 15, 1869. She resides in Nickerson, Kan.
536. II. ABRAM R., b. Jan. 24, 1816; d. Sept. 21, 1852; m. March, 1840, Samantha Fuller, who d. Nov., 1852. They lived in Lowell, Ind.
537. III. HORATIO NELSON RICE, b. Jan. 26, 1818; m. Jan. 23, 1843, Phebe Eliza Kenyon. They reside in Lowell, Ind.
538. IV. CAROLINE B., b. Dec. 13, 1819; m. Oct. 24, 1839, Joseph Chester Smith, b. March 13, 1816; d. July 16, 1873; m (2) March 2, 1885, James Henry Koff. They reside in South Troupsburgh, N. Y.

539. v. EUNICE ROSETTA, b. Dec. 21, 1821, m. May 12, 1842, William Onion, Jr., b. Sept. 4, 1822; d. Dec. 19, 1847; m. (2) March 27, 1848, Hezekiah Gridley, who d. Aug., 1854; m. (3) March 29, 1855, Charles Smith. She resides in Eureka, Ill.

540. vi. RHODA ALMEDA, b. Feb. 22, 1824; m. April 26, 1843, Horace Kellogg Smith, b. Nov. 30, 1801; d. Jan. 22, 1853; m. (2) Oct. 1, 1854, Ithamar Bump, b. Jan. 28, 1825. They reside in Troupsburgh, N. Y.

541. vii. NANCY, b. Feb. 11, 1825; d. 1844.

542. viii. WILLIAM WALLACE, b. Nov. 1, 1827; m. Oct. 31, 1852, Harriet Malvina Judd, b. Aug. 29, 1835. They reside in Laporte, Ind.

543. ix. HULDAH, b. March 16, 1831; m. Oct. 27, 1849, Edwin Hamilton Judd, b. Feb. 22, 1829. They reside at St. Anne, Ill.

544. x. MARY JANE, b. July 23, 1833; m. Nov. 22, 1849, Hamilton Perry, b. April 9, 1822; d. June 16, 1879. She resides at St. Anne, Ill.

121.

Harvey Resseguie Nichols, born in Rensselaer County, N. Y., May 9, 1802; died in Manchester, Mich., Oct. 4, 1876. He married in Fenner, N. Y., Jan. 13, 1824, Nancy Ann Raymond, daughter of Jacob and Anna (Sanford) Raymond, of that town. She was born in Newtown, Conn., Feb. 8, 1802; died at Grass Lake, Mich., Jan. 16, 1879.

Mr. Nichols removed with his parents to Fenner, in his infancy. When about sixteen he commenced teaching school and clerking in a country store. About the time of his marriage he embarked in mercantile business for a short time. He removed to Penn Yan, Yates County, in 1832, and lived there three years, during which time he was employed as captain of a canal boat running between Albany and Buffalo. In Sept., 1835, he removed to Ann Arbor, Mich., and the next spring to Grass Lake, where he bought a farm upon which he remained until 1866. In the fall of that year he removed to Norvell and engaged in mercantile business, but two years later returned to his farm. Shortly after this, his health beginning to fail, he retired from active life, and went to live with his son in Manchester, Mich., where the remainder of his life was passed.

CHILDREN. (*Fifth Generation.*)

545. I. ANNA MARIA, b. Feb. 25, 1826; d. July 27, 1857.
546. II. MATILDA, b. Feb. 11, 1830; d. July 6, 1851.
547. III. CHARLES HARVEY, b. Dec. 1, 1834; m. Jan. 1, 1861, Augusta Ely Greenman, b. April 26, 1838. They reside in Manchester, Mich.

122.

Nathaniel Resseguie, born in Sharon, Schoharie County, N. Y., Oct. 8, 1784; died in Canajoharie, N. Y., Oct. 3, 1850. He married in Sharon, March 16, 1818, Sophia Barnes, daughter of Dan and Hannah (Lord) Barnes of Columbia County. She died in Canajoharie July 8, 1862. Mr. Resseguie removed from Sharon to Canajoharie April 1, 1834. He was a farmer and cattle dealer.

CHILDREN. (*Fifth Generation.*)

548.   I.   INFANT, not named, b. Feb. 10, 1819; d. Feb. 14, 1819.
549.   II.   DAN, b. June 6, 1822; m. April 27, 1848, Eve Maria Leroy, who d. Feb. 6, 1879. He resides in Canajoharie, N. Y.
550.   III.   JOHN, b. April 7, 1825; m. July 8, 1863, Martha Wemple. They reside in Canajoharie, N. Y.
551.   IV.   MARY ANN, b. Aug. 18, 1828; d. July 1, 1830.
552.   V.   EPHRAIM, b. Jan. 24, 1831; m. March 21, 1855, Lydia Melissa Drum. They reside at Leesville, N. Y.

123.

Mary Resseguie, born Aug. 28, 1786; died in 1855. She married in Sharon, N. Y., in 1814, Aldrich Wyley Barrett, who was born in Woodstock, Conn., April 3, 1779, and died March 18, 1847. Mr. Barrett removed to Sharon at the age of three years; in 1826 went to Covington, Genesee County, N. Y., and in 1838 settled in Pavillion, Wyoming County, which thenceforth remained his home. He was a deacon in the Universalist Church. In addition to farming he carried on the business of shoemaking.

CHILDREN. (*Fifth Generation.*)

553.   I.   CALISTA, b. July 19, 1815; m. May 8, 1833, Mark Neill, who d. May 6, 1866. She resides in Carlton, N. Y.
554.   II.   ANN ELIZABETH, b. April 3, 1816; m. Oct. 19, 1837, Nelson Johnson, b. May 11, 1816; d. July 4, 1878. She resides in Albion, N. Y.
555.   III.   ARMENIA, b. April 19, 1824; m. Sept. 6, 1845, Riley·Merrilis Fox, b. Oct. 28, 1825; d. Jan. 19, 1873. She resides in Castile, N. Y.
556.   IV.   REBECCA, b. Oct. 4, 1828; m. Jan. 18, 1853, Samuel Morey Forbes. They reside at Castile.

124.

Anna Resseguie, born may 10, 1788; died in Sycamore, Ill., Oct. 21, 1872. She married Robert Mitchell, a farmer, who died in Sycamore, Dec. 14, 1865.

CHILDREN. (*Fifth Generation.*)

557. I. LOVELL ARAMEL, b. Nov. 6, 1817; m. 1850, Anna Elizabeth Pitcher. They reside at Anamosa, Ia.
558. II. WILLIAM HENRY HARRISON, b. Oct. 13, 1819; d. Dec. 9, 1884; m. March 3, 1853, Mary A. Atwood. He lived in Mayfield (Sycamore), Ill.
559. III. HARRIET LOUISA, b. Feb. 4, 1821; m. July 3, 1844, Zelotes Bingham Mayo, who d. March 7, 1879. She resides in Sycamore, Ill.
560. IV. NORMAN NORTON, b. May 25, 1826; d. May 14, 1880; m. Sept. 1, 1858, Kate Erskine. She resides in Parsons, Kan.

125.

Phœbe Resseguie, born June 25, 1792; married James Phelps, son of Addison Phelps, who was born in Greene County, N. Y. He was a farmer, and lived in Yorkshire, N. Y. No further record can be secured.

CHILDREN. (*Fifth Generation.*)

561. I. AUSTIN, b. Feb. 22, 1822; d. Jan. 9, 1887; m. July 8, 1840, Louisa Jennette Watson, who d. Nov. 2, 1860; m. (2d) June 6, 1861, Rosina Olney. He lived at Alexander, N. Y.
562. II. WILLIAM ADDISON, b. April 6, 1825; m. Jan. 13, 1848, Mary Jane Lippitt. They live at Rockton, Ill.
563. III. LOVISA, b. Feb. 8, 1828; m. Feb. 13, 1847, Hartley W. Fox, b. June 19, 1827. They reside at Freedom, N. Y.
564. IV. JAMES HARVEY, b. Jan. 6, 1831; d. April 6, 1864; m. June 11, 1851, Clarrissa E. Barrus. He lived at Elton, N. Y.
565. V. PHŒBE LOUISA, b. Nov. 15, 1833; m. Dec. 25, 1853, Jacob Lane Strong, b. March 20, 1826. They live at Freedom, N. Y.

126.

*****John Resseguie**, born in Connecticut, May 17, 1793; died in Sharon, N. Y., Sept. 10, 1856. He married in Sharon, Nov. 30, 1819, Eve Anthony, daughter of Jacob and Eve (Piser) Anthony of that town, who was born Jan. 30, 1804, and is still living in Sharon. Mr. Resseguie was a farmer; a deacon in the Lutheran church at Argusville, for many years. Though many times importuned by his townsmen, he would never accept public office.

** All the descendants of John Resseguie (126) have adopted *Ressegieu* as the orthography of the name.*

CHILDREN. (*Fifth Generation.*)

566. I. JOHN HENRY, b. March 17, 1821; m. Jan. 16, 1850, Henrietta M. Sweatman. They reside in Sharon, N. Y.
567. II. JACOB ANTHONY, M. D., b. Sept. 2, 1822; m. Dec. 31, 1844, Lydia Kilts. They reside in Sioux City, Ia.
568. III. MARY CATHARINE, b. Feb. 5, 1825; m. March 15, 1855, Dwight Merril Foster, b. Dec. 31, 1827. They reside in Cincinnatus, N. Y.
569. IV. JAMES, b. Jan. 3, 1827. Resides in Cleopatra, Mo.; unmarried.
570. V. EVELINE, b. Jan. 28, 1829; d. Jan. 18, 1865; m. May 28, 1856, Levi Maricle, b. June 13, 1832; d. Oct. 10, 1865. They lived at Marathon, N. Y.
571. VI. ELIZA ABIGAIL, b. Sept. 23, 1831. Resides in Sharon, N. Y.
572. VII. AGNES ELLEN, b. Feb. 7, 1833; m. Oct. 3, 1886, George Winne. They reside at Root, N. Y.
573. VIII. DAVID WASHINGTON, b. July 4, 1835; d. Sept. 10, 1836.
574. IX. GEORGE FOX, b. June 2, 1837; m. May 19, 1873, Lotitia Montange. They reside in Sharon.
575. X. ANNA, b. April 12, 1839; m. Jan. 25, 1872, Oscar Courtney, b. Dec. 4, 1834. They reside in Marathon, N. Y.
576. XI. LUCINDA, b. March 5, 1846; m. Oct. 10, 1865, Wellington Crounse, b. May 27, 1845.

127.

Elizabeth Resseguie, born in Sharon, N. Y., May 30, 1795; died in Sweden, Monroe County, Aug. 31, 1869. She married in Sharon, Jan. 23, 1817, Samuel Vibber Way, son of Samuel Way of Springfield, Otsego County, N. Y., who was born in Colchester, Conn., May 7, 1792, and died in Sweden, May 25, 1883. Mr. Way removed with his parents when three years old to Otsego County, and in 1816 to Sweden, then in the wilderness. In middle life he held the offices of elder and trustee in the Congregational church, also various town offices.

CHILDREN. (*Fifth Generation.*)

577. I. ALONZO BIGELOW, b. June 6, 1818; d. Feb. 17, 1840.
578. II. HARVEY, b. April 27, 1820; m. March 11, 1842, Amelia C. Young. They reside in Sweden, N. Y.
579. III. HARRIET, b. April 27, 1820; m. Jan. 9, 1841, Lorenzo D. Bangs, b. July 19, 1815. They reside in Churchville (town of Riga), N. Y.
580. IV. JOHN RESSEGUIE, b. Dec. 3, 1821; d. Sept. 18, 1840.
581. V. ELIZABETH, b. Sept. 6, 1825; d. Oct. 29, 1834.
582. VI. GEORGE H., b. Sept. 30, 1827; m. Jan. 11, 1854, Clara Eliza Chappell. They reside in Sweden, N. Y.

583. VII. SARAH, b. Oct. 18, 1831; m. March 15, 1854, Elisha Locke, b. Dec. 11, 1830; d. June 20, 1876. She resides in Sweden, N. Y.
584. VIII. MARY ELIZABETH, b. June 17, 1834; d. July 27, 1863; m. Feb. 17, 1858, Dr. John Barker Wilford, who d. June 17, 1881.

132.

Betsey Resseguie, born June, 1781; died in Ridgefield, Conn., Feb. 10, 1867. She married, about 1801, Alpheus Canfield, who was born in South Salem, N. Y., about 1779, and died in Ridgefield, Nov. 25, 1842. Mr. Canfield was a farmer and builder, and removed to Ridgefield, from his native place, in childhood.

CHILDREN. (*Fifth Generation.*)

585. I. RUFUS, b. Dec. 3, 1802; m. Dec. 22, 1823, Polly Northrop, b. Sept. 14, 1801; d. Nov. 21, 1873. He lives (1884) in New Brunswick, N. J.
586. II. ROSWELL, b. April 8, 1804; d. Dec., 1876; m. Nov., 1828, Julia Olmstead. They lived in Seymour, Conn.
587. III. SARAH, b. June 29, 1808; d. Feb. 16, 1879; m. Sept. 30, 1828, Jesse Covert, b. 1799; d. June, 1836; m. (2d) about 1844, Justus Miller; m. (3d) Benjamin Corser. She lived in Ridgefield, Conn.
588. IV. JULIA ANN, b. July 17, 1809; d. March 26, 1884; m. April 4, 1828, Joseph Ingersoll, b. Sept. 18, 1807; d. June 25, 1868.
589. V. SAMUEL, b. July 15, 1811; m. June 30, 1839, Catharine Dunning, b. Dec. 26, 1811. They reside in Georgetown, Conn.
590. VI. WILLIAM, b. June 20, 1813; d. Sept. 15, 1854; m. Aug. 17, 1836, Ann Dusenberry. She resides in Brooklyn, N. Y.
591. VII. ELIZA, b. March 28, 1817; d. May 12, 1847; m. Oct., 1836, Joseph Shadrach Ferris, b. May 30, 1815. He resides in Milford, Conn.
592. VIII. GOULD RANSLEY, b. March 19, 1819; d. Aug. 20, 1838.
593. IX. HARRIET, b. Sept. 11, 1823; m. Dec. 24, 1843, Walter Parsons, b. Dec. 25, 1821. They reside in Washington, D. C.

134.

Abijah Resseguie, born in Ridgefield, Conn., March 26, 1791; died there April 16, 1887, aged ninety-six years. He married, Feb. 1, 1829, Anne Keeler, daughter of * Timothy and Esther

---

* "Squire Timothy Keeler was born in 1769, and died in 1815. He was a representative in the General Assembly, justice of the peace, and postmaster for many years." — *S. G. Goodrich* (Peter Parley).

(Kellogg) Keeler, of Ridgefield. She was born Nov. 9, 1787, and died in Ridgefield Dec. 23, 1862. Mr. Resseguie was for many years the proprietor of the "old Keeler tavern," which, under the management of his father-in-law, 'Squire Keeler, was widely famous as a hospitable hostelry. The old tavern sign was long since taken down, but it may not be uninteresting to quote a few brief lines from " Peter Parley's Recollections of a Lifetime," in support of the reputation once accorded it : " He who wishes to eat with a relish that the Astor House, or Morley's, or the Grand Hotel de Louvre cannot give, should go to Ridgefield and put himself under the care of Mrs. Resseguie. When you go there — as go you must — do not forget to order ham and eggs, for they are such as we ate in our childhood. As to blackberry and huckleberry pies, and similar good gifts, you will find them just such as our mother made fifty years ago, when these bounties of Providence were included in the prayer, 'Give us this day our daily bread,' and were a worthy answer to such a petition." A cannon-ball, shot by the British during the Revolutionary War, may still be seen firmly imbedded in the northeast corner post of the house.

The following interesting and comprehensive account of Mr. Resseguie is taken from the Ridgefield *Press:*

"The soul of the venerable and respected landlord, Abijah Resseguie, has left its earthly habitation and gone before. The fruit has fully ripened and is gathered into the storehouse.

"Mr. Resseguie was a descendant of staunch old Huguenot stock, remarkable for longevity of life and sturdiness of manhood. In the bloody massacre of St. Bartholomew (1572) many of his ancestors perished. He was ninety-six years of age at the time of his death. Notwithstanding his old age, a week before he died, in a chat with a neighbor, he seemed to enjoy the witticisms and general conversation as much as he would have done in his younger days. He astonished his friends with his wonderful gift of memory. He could recall any important event in his own life or the general history of his country.

"While men who live but half his ripe years become 'old-fogyish' in their notions, Mr. Resseguie was always up with the times, and took deep interest in all current doings and events, local and general. He believed in progress, and was always watching as carefully the many improvements in 'old Ridge- field' as did his younger neighbors.

"Mr. Resseguie was a man who never indulged in tobacco in any form ; he was not straight-laced, by any means, in his manner of living, though he believed in temperance. He knew how to cater to the traveling public in the cuisine line, and he could enjoy a good dinner, too. He never exercised fanat- icism in matters which to him seemed right. He was far from being narrow in his views, and, while enjoying discussion of a question, he would always concede the point when worsted. To sum up,— he was as much unlike the vast majority of elderly country people of our time as is day unlike night. He might have been called, with semblance of truth, a young man of progressive ideas in the guise of an elderly gentleman.

"At an early age, Mr. Resseguie showed evidence of a mechanical bent of mind; and it was not a mistake when, in his fifteenth year, after having acquired a fair education, he was apprenticed to a carriage-maker, John Watrous, who lived in a cottage occupying the site of the present home of Mr. Charles Brown. His employer, perceiving inventive genius in the lad, soon made him a valuable assistant during their 'off hours,' in contriving labor-saving tools for the trade, and even in attempting to solve that most perplexing of all enigmas, perpetual motion. And here we might parenthetically state that Mr. Resseguie, from boyhood to the month of his death, studied with deep concern all the great inventions of the past century,— the steamboat, the locomotive, the electric telegraph, and, in Edison's time, the later wonderful achievements. When he visited the Brooklyn bridge three or four years ago, he stood on that mammoth structure for an hour examining into and inquiring about the principles of the cable road. At this time he visited the New York Stock Exchange, and expressed satisfaction in noting the many wonderful achievements in modern architecture.

"After serving his apprenticeship, he continued to pursue his trade in the town of his birth, and for years he was the respected head of the firm of Resseguie & Olmstead, doing a thriving carriage business. The firm shipped vehicles South and West, and supplied Orange County, N. Y., with hundreds of wagons of Ridgefield manufacture.

"In the year 1828 Mr. Resseguie began to realize that it was not good to live alone; and, like thousands of his fellows, discovered the 'one ideal of his heart,' and Miss Anna, daughter of Landlord Keeler,— who 'kept tavern' in the very house in which our subject passed away — was led to the hymeneal altar. When Mr. Keeler died the hotel fell into the hands of Mr. Resseguie, and for sixty years our late venerable resident has been known as Landlord Resseguie. Mrs. Resseguie died in 1862.

"Mr. Resseguie never courted notoriety or prominence, and whatever official position he held was thrust upon him. Like all other respectable citizens of a country town, he was an available candidate for town offices, and filled several such positions during his earlier life. He was also elected to the General Assembly in 1847, and gave satisfaction to his constituents. In general politics he was conservative, but voted with the Whigs, and afterward with the Republicans.

"Being a man of strict integrity, honor, and principle, Mr. Resseguie was a faithful adherent of his religious creed. He early connected himself with St. Stephen's Church, this village, and took active part in all that society's doings throughout the best years of his life. For twenty years he was a warden, filling that office acceptably to within a year of his demise.

"It was deeply interesting and exceedingly amusing to the neighbor and friend to listen to the aged landlord's anecdotes and incidents connected with his career, many of which give so true a picture of Ridgefield in earlier times. He remembered distinctly to have heard the church bells toll on the day of Washington's death. He was then only eight years of age. He was a witness of the last flogging which took place in Ridgefield — that barbarous punishment so repulsive to modern times; and he often related how cruel was the scene of the whipping-post, and of the rejoicing of the people when that relic of barbarism was abolished.

"Words fail to give more than the slightest idea of the geniality and sunshine which hallowed the departed innkeeper's existence. He never looked on the dark side. He was always ready to enjoy a witty story, and as a story-teller he was always popular on the long winter evenings, while the company of friends, with the quota of travelers, were gathered about the old-time fireplace with its crackling logs. There was no end to his humor.

"To show how sturdy he was in his old age, it may not be amiss to state that he attended the Centennial Exposition at Philadelphia in 1876, and that, at eighty years of age, he tired out the younger members of his party sight-seeing in Washington.

"Within a few years he seemed deeply interested in the Mackay-Bennett cable, and interviewed every caller whom he thought might have been posted on the subject. Mr. Resseguie is conceded by the fraternity to have been the oldest Free Mason in the country, he having joined the order in the year 1812. Because of this fact he had acquired a national reputation.

"The funeral of Mr. Resseguie was attended at his late residence on Tuesday, at 11 o'clock, A. M., Rev. W. W. Leete officiating. The house was filled with sympathizing friends, and the very few who remain to claim the closer tie of kinship with the deceased. Several beautiful floral designs were about the house, some of them presented by those who sojourn here during the summer, and who had learned, like the rest of us, to appreciate the cheerful presence of the one who has now gone from our village no more to return. The service, in keeping with Mr. Resseguie's taste and at his daughter's request, was simple and brief. After reading from the Episcopal service to the end of the Scriptural selection, Mr. Leete remarked somewhat as follows:

"'I turn from the sustained dignity of this noble service of burial, which, in its lines, emphasize the solemn thoughts of death, judgment, and the life to come, as also the sweeter comfort of Gospel hope, to speak but one word of the departed. As we take out from this ancient homestead the venerable form which has so long been a tenant here, it would seem strange to allow that word to remain unspoken. Your hearts are all occupied with it, and I would not divert them by mentioning something new.

"'It is no ordinary life which has closed. When we reflect on the period through which that life has extended, we feel the force of this remark. His years almost covered the age of the constitution of this republic, his eyes beholding the light of every presidential administration. He saw thrones tremble, and heard of "war and rumors of wars" on every continent. Agitations of thought and social reformations of the most extensive kind have affected the world since he took his place in it. The services and inventions which contribute now so materially to the comforts of living have come to their perfection under his notice. No one was more desirous of understanding them or ready to acknowledge their merits than he. His life has thus run through all the changes of our busy nineteenth century like a golden thread. The facts and events which group themselves along the line and are even associated with his person crowd our memory to-day, and might engage our attention very long.

"'But the quality of his life, not its duration or the remarkable events which came in connection with it, makes it most precious to us who gather to-day. He was a rare spirit. A few moments' conversation with him revealed mental and social qualities of a very high order, while the sweetness of his character was a reminder of the Divine Master whom he had learned to obey.

"'Sprung from the blood of the Huguenots, he exercised toward all, both in speech and action, that sweet charity which was so wanting in the men who persecuted his ancestors beyond the sea. These facts and qualities, not to mention his public position as the keeper of this house, which has already taken its place in written history, gave him somewhat the position of a patriarch. He seemed as a father to all of us who passed up and down by his door. He belonged to every one, as did not other persons in our streets. As townsmen, we took pride in him, and almost the first question of the stranger was about the health of the old gentleman who kept the hotel. To know Ridgefield was to know him, and, in an absolute sense, to know him was to know Ridgefield, for none knew so much about it or had a greater interest in the past and future. His memory, very accurate and lively down to the last, was an unfailing storehouse, open to the searcher for hid treasures, and some of us will regret to-day that we have not more often resorted there.

"'And now he is gone, like all our fathers who were but pilgrims and strangers. We come as children to mingle the tears of affection and to testify how much we loved him.

"Take him for all in all,
We shall not look upon his like again."

"'Genial and vivacious, but gentle and pure and patient, maintaining these traits even to the hour of death, after the lapse of almost a century, the inmates of this house, who have watchfully ministered to every want, and the wider circle in which he was held, have never had occasion to do aught but thank God for this marked exception to the statement of Scripture as to the number of man's days.

"'I will not say more. I would not voice an eulogy, which would be to him, of all men, most distasteful. And yet, with less than I have spoken our responsive hearts cannot be satisfied, as we pronounce above the casket of the dear old man the painful word, farewell.'"

CHILD. (*Fifth Generation.*)

594. I. ANNE, b. 1830; resides in Ridgefield, Conn.

137.

Eliza Resseguie, born in Ridgefield, Conn., May 7, 1800; died there Oct. 30, 1852. She married Nelson Hallock.

CHILD. (*Fifth Generation.*)

595. I. SILAS, resided (1873) at or near Kaneville, Ill.

INDEX.

Descendants and family connections referred to by number; all others by pages.

Ager, James,	235	Barrett, Rebecca, . . . 556
Allen, Alonzo, . . .	531	" Sarah, ... 41
" Eliza, . . .	53	Barrus, Clarissa E., . . . 564
" John, . . .	53	Beach, Merritt, . . . 511
" Samuel Peter, . .	266	Beardslee, John, . . . 516
" Simon, . . .	218	" Rebecca, . . . 107
Ambler, William Aaron, .	377	Becker, Mary, . . . 330
Ammerman, Albert, . .	406	Beckwith, Jedediah, . . 36
Anderson, Alexander Marshall, .	514	Beecher, Lois Amanda, . . 451
Andrews, Sewall, . .	409	" Mary, . . . 446
Anthony, Eve, . . .	126	" Clarinda, . . 448
" Jacob, . . .	126	Beekman, Alida, . . . 162
Arcularius, Louisa, . .	426	Belden, Azor, Page 20.
Ashton, Watson, . .	336	" John, Pages 12, 20.
Atwood, Mary A., . .	558	" Thankful, . . 2
Austin, Almeda, . .	318	Bellomont, Lord, Page 11.
Avery, Lucy, . . .	48	Benedict, Benjamin, . . . 96
" Punderson, . .	48	" Benjamin Smith, 462
Ayres, Martha Swem, . .	283	" Edward, . . . 458
" Matthew, . . .	449	" Edwin, . . . 459
		" Eli S., . . . 394
Bailey, Adelia, . . .	250	" Emily, . . . 457
" Mary, . . .	369	" Jane Ann, . . 460
Baird, Rev. Charles W., Page 11.		" Jesse, . . . 96
Bangs, Lorenzo D., . .	579	" John Harvey, . . 460
Barber, Angenette, . .	259	" Mary, . . . 461
" Jemima, . .	393	" Matthew, Page 18.
Barnes, Dan, . . .	122	" Thankful, . . 101
" Levina, . . .	48	Bennem, Lydia Ann, . . 298
" Miranda, . . .	417	Bessey, Samuel Harvey, Jr., . 343
" Sophia, . . .	122	Betts, Samuel, Page 20.
Barrett, Aldrich Wyley, .	123	Bingham, Nancy Celestia, . . 153
" Ann Elizabeth, .	554	Blachly, Phebe Amelia, . . 298
" Armenia, . .	555	Blackman, Eunice, . . . 12
" Calista, . . .	553	Blakeley, Susan Angeline, . . 150
" Nancy, . . .	41	Blye, Alonzo D., . . . 524

Bonaparte, Napoleon, Page 43.		Caldwell, Joseph, Page 62.		
Bontecou, Pierre,	1	Camp, Anna,		25
" Sara,	1	Canfield, Abel, Jr.,		107
" Timothy, Page 12.		" Alanson Norman,		508
Botsford, Eliza,	218	" Alpheus,		132
" Henry,	217	" Anna,		106
" William,	44	" Eliza,		591
Bouton, Phebe,	86	" Gould Ransley,		592
" Sarah,	87	" Harriet,		593
" Seth,	18	" Isaac,		106
" Seth,	88	" Jane Ann,		509
Bowling, Margaret Susan,	489	" Julia Ann,		588
Bradbury, Elizabeth,	105	" Ralph Edwin,		510
" William,	105	" Rebecca Sophia,		511
Bradley, Daniel, Page 37.		" Roswell,		586
" Sally,	148	" Rufus,		585
" Sarah Stebbins,	100	" Samuel,		589
Brailey, Abigail,	25	" Sarah,		587
Briggs, Benjamin,	144	" William,		590
Brockway, Almira,	248	" William Nelson,		507
Brown, Amelia,	251	Carpenter, Elvira Elizabeth,		321
" Charles, Page 82.		" Esther M.,		203
" Dahyler,	222	" Frances,		291
" Elizabeth,	313	" Polly Mariah,		67
" Hiram Sanford,	418	" Robert Nason,		67
" John,	65	Case, Aaron,		58
" Julie,	340	" Mary,		58
" Lydia,	65	Chappell, Clara Eliza,		582
" Rufus,	445	Chaffee, Jane,		306
Brownson, Laura Lucinda,	520	Chilson, Jehiel,		441
Bump, Annis,	527	Childs, Lydia,		149
" Harvey Resseguie Nichols,	528	Cheney, William Alonzo,		407
" Ithamar,	540	Claggett, Stephen,		284
" Jacob,	113	Clark, Betsey,		67
" Mary,	526	Clinton, Rhoda,		448
Burney, William Joseph,	280	Colburn, Elizabeth,		62
Burns, Mary,	54	Cole, Allee,		384
Burr, Andrew, Page 18.		" Almira,		345
" David, Pages 14, 18.		" Alonzo,		367
Burrhus, Alonzo,	435	" Angeline,		357
Burt, Betsey,	129	" Augustus,		368
" David,	26	" Augustus,		372
" David,	131	" Asa,		71
" Hannah,	130	" Asa,		347
" Seaborn,	128	" Betsey,		345
Bushnell, Lydia,	416	" Caroline,		371
Button, Alonzo,	230	" Charles,		373

Cole, Charles,	344	Cole, Timothy, . . . 72
" Charles Edward,	340	" William, . . . 366
" Curtis,	74	Collamer, Warren Barnabas, . 353
" Curtis,	348	" Warren Barnabas, . 356
" David,	66	Collinot, Marguerite, . . 1
" Edwin,	358	Collins, Prudence C., . . . 327
" Eli,	339	Comstock, Jemima, . . . 215
" Eliza, .	377	Cone, Almira, . . . 248
" Eliza Ann, .	356	Conrad, George, . . . 208
" Elizabeth, .	66	Cook, Adeline, . . . 221
" Emily,	375	" Augustin, . . . 322
" Emory,	350	Coon, David, . . . 44
" Esther Mary,	343	Cooper, William Scureman, . 413
" Frederick Victor,	386	Copp, John, Page 12.
" George,	342	Corey, Joseph, . . . 64
" George,	351	" Lucy, . . . 64
" Harmon,	394	Corning, Lucinda Susanna, . 264
" Harriet,	349	Corser, Benjamin, . . 587
" Hattie,	380	Courtney, Oscar, . . 575
" Henry,	369	Covert, Jane, . . . 424
" Henry,	383	" Jesse, . . . 587
" Ira,	71	Crane, Amariah, . . . 62
" Ira,	378	" Catharine, . . 347
" James,	456	" Eunice, . . . 62
" James Sturges, .	365	" Thomas, Page 34.
" Jane, .	354	Crandall, Sarah Thurston, . . 404
" Jane, .	376	Cranson, Sybil, . . . 24
" Julia Ann, .	364	Crouch, Cynthia, . . . 304
" Lester Sherman,	385	" Daniel Resseguie, . 303
" Lucy Ann, .	374	" Emily Semantha, . . 329
" Lydia,	71	" Esther, . . . 302
" Lydia Anna,	381	" Hannah Field, . 305
" Mabel,	39	" John, . . . 308
" Mary, .	353	" Joshua, . . . 59
" Mary Eliza,	370	" Samuel, . . . 307
" Mary Esther,	379	" William Harrison, . 306
" Melvina,	333	Crounse, Wellington, . . 576
" Minerva,	355	Culver, Tacy, . . . 518
" Molly,	70	Curtis, Mary, . . . 7
" Polly,	346	" Nathan, . . . 7
" Ruth Hamilton,	271	
" Sally, .	73	Darby, Andrew J., . . . 433
" Sally, .	352	Darling, Harriet, . . . 450
" Samuel,	75	Darrin, Daniel, Jr., . . 387
" Sherman, .	76	Dauchey, Jane, . . . 464
" Theodore, .	382	" Jeremiah, . . . 98
" Thomas,	16	" Samuel S., . . . 463
" Thomas,	70	Davis, Caleb, . . . 199

Davis, Mary,	462
Delavergne, Thurza,	320
Denio, Francis G.,	421
" Ruth Garnet,	507
Denney, Betsey Ann,	212
Denton, Lydia,	193
" Trumbull,	530
De Reemer, Mary Ann,	143
Dewey, Israel,	80
" Mary,	80
Dickey, Walter,	209
Dikeman, Mary,	74
Disbrow, Almira,	237
" Fannie Ketura,	242
" Freelove,	43
" Justus,	43
Doty, Polly,	82
" Prince,	82
Downes, Benjamin Philo,	505
Drake, Ella,	335
Drum, Lydia Melissa,	552
Dryer, Clarina Jane,	282
Dunham, Matilda Withers,	174
Dunning, Catharine,	589
Durkee, Benjamin Smith,	535
Dusenberry, Ann,	590
Dusinberre, Phineas Rice,	380
Dyson, John,	193
Eagleston, Deborah,	75
Eastman, George Nial,	277
" George Nial,	278
" Lois,	276
Eaton, Rachel,	251
Edes, Frances Calista,	263
Edmonds, Julia Ann,	360
Edwards, Annette,	234
" ——,	437
England, John Wesley,	290
Erskine, Kate,	560
Fancher, Thankful,	71
Felter, Matthew,	444
Felton, Mary Ann,	187
Ferris, Harriet Newel,	267
" Joseph Shadrach,	591
Ferry, Subrina,	118
Field, Mary,	310

Field, Mary A.,	366
" Spafford,	61
Fields, Joseph Elnathan,	364
Fithian, Elizabeth Sinnickson,	481
Floyd, Elizabeth,	105
Folliot, Sarah,	27
Foot, Sarah,	83
Forbes, Jemima Clement,	392
" Samuel Morey,	556
Forster, John,	89
" Mary,	89
Fort, John, Jr.,	527
Foster, Dwight Merril,	568
" Duke, Page 24.	
Fountain, Matthew, Page 20.	
Fowler, Clarissa,	358
Fox, Hartley W.,	563
" Riley Merrills,	555
Frisbie, Samuel,	519
Fuller, Ruth Garnet,	507
" Samantha,	536
Ganung, John, Page 24.	
" Riley,	44
Garlick, Sarah,	23
Gaskill, Lydia,	66
Gault, Calvin,	408
Gaylord, Ruth,	21
Gereaux, Charles Louis,	195
Gibbs, Jonathan Andrew,	346
Gifford, Ebenezer,	299
Gilbert, Egbert W.,	374
Gilman, Mary Eleanor,	311
Gleason, James Hubbard,	176
Goodrich, Adaline,	264
" Samuel G., Page 80.	
Goodwin, Sarah,	223
Grant, Adaline S.,	148
" Gen. Ulysses S., Page 45.	
Graves, Abigail,	213
Gray, Alexander,	267
" Betsey Ann,	266
" Caroline,	265
" Caroline,	270
" Edward,	51
" George Edward,	264
" Joel,	51
" Joel,	269

INDEX

Gray, Noah Duane,	271
" Sara Jane,	268
Green, Anginette T.,	340
" Nathaniel Warren,	310
Greenman, Augusta Ely,	547
Gregory, Alanson Peck,	469
" Eli,	101
" John Alexander,	471
" Nathan,	101
" Nathan Benedict,	470
Gridley, Hezekiah,	439
Grimes, Joseph,	453
" Sara Abigail,	454
Groesbeck, Isaac,	294
Gros, Maria Philipena,	159
Gunn, Mary,	31
Hall, Kate Frances,	386
" Thomas,	141
Hallock, Nelson,	137
" Silas,	595
Halpin, John, Jr.,	312
Hanford, Thomas, Page 12.	
Harden, Joseph,	255
Harrison, George Justus,	466
Hart, Amasa Philip,	252
" Laura,	253
Hatch, Ellen Climan,	272
Hawley, Thomas, Page 24.	
Heacock, Ezra, Pages 14, 18, 19.	
Hendrick, Martin,	443
Hendrickson, A. D.,	411
Herrick, Harriet,	447
" Minerva Hopkins,	452
" Ozias Bissell,	182
Hervey, James Aigin,	497
Hess, Aaron,	57
" Catharine,	110
" Cordelia,	293
" Deidrick,	110
" Edwin Lee,	291
" Jacob,	440
" John,	54
" John,	57
" John,	292
" Margaret Ann,	54
Hickok, Ezra, Pages 14, 18, 19.	
Hicks, Joseph E.,	424

Hill, Rebecca Isaacs,	378
Hills, Kate,	134
Hine, Isaac,	140
Hitchcock, Mary,	430
Hochstrasser, Anna E.,	170
Holmes, Daphne,	142
Hotchkiss, George,	516
Houghtaling, Harriet Smith,	515
Howe, Charles Corydon,	268
Hoyt, Benjamin, Page 18.	
" Maria,	458
" William Rockwell,	465
Hubbard, Caleb,	445
Hubbell, Nathan, Page 20.	
" Peter,	93
" Peter, Page 20.	
" Sara,	93
" Thad., Page 21.	
Hull, Esther,	109
Humphrey, Polly,	93
Hunt, Lovina,	323
Hurd, Asa,	441
Hurlbutt, Lewis,	76
" Susan,	76
Ingersoll, Joseph,	588
Jackson, John Robert,	331
" Laverna,	344
Jacobs, Mary Jane,	454
Jelliff, William H.,	341
Jennings, Julia,	93
" Richard,	93
Jewett, Elizabeth,	466
" Mary,	465
" Nathan,	99
" Thaddeus,	99
Johnson, Nelson,	534
Judd, Edwin Hamilton,	543
" Harriet Malvina,	542
Judson, Eunice,	7
" Phebe,	103
Kane, Amanda,	417
Keeler, Anne,	134
" Daniel,	10
" Esther,	10
" Mary,	10

Keeler, Ruhamah,	.	29
" Samuel, Page 12.		
" Timothy,	.	134
Keeney, Horatio Seymour,	.	228
Kellogg, Esther,	.	134
Kelsey, Huldah,	.	118
" Reuben,	.	118
Kenyon, Phebe Eliza,	.	537
Kilts, Lydia,	.	567
Kimberly, Ephraim, Page 21.		
King, Mary Helen,	.	279
" Mercy,	.	66
Kirkham, Joshua Henry,	.	287
Knowlton, Sargent,	.	400
Knox, Albert Rutson,	.	423
" George W.,	.	532
Laborie, Jacques, Page 11.		
Lamb, Prudence B.,	.	518
Lambert, David, Page 19.		
Lamson, Hannah,	.	106
Lanning, Isaac,	.	422
Larkin, Hiram Stephen,	.	254
Lathrop, Abigail,	.	213
Lawrence, Martin Puffer,	.	309
Leach, Cornelia Louisa,	.	145
" Samuel Kidder,	.	503
Lee, Abigail,	.	14
" John,	.	14
" Thomas,	.	206
Leete, Lydia Meigs,	.	49
" Noah,	.	49
" Rev. W. W., Page 83.		
LeFevre, Martin Richtmyer,	.	338
Lennon, Martha,	.	447
Lent, Milton G.,	.	371
Leroy, Eve Maria,	.	549
LeRoy, Peter Francis,	.	146
Lewis, Celestia Ann,	.	337
" Deborah,	.	50
" Hannah Minerva,	.	338
" Hiram,	.	69
" Joseph,	.	69
" Mary Maria,	.	336
Lindsley, Daniel Hall,	.	319
Lines, Mercy,	.	508
Lippitt, Mary Jane,	.	562
Lobdell, ——,	.	37
Lobdell, Abigail,	.	37
" Maria,	.	173
Locke, Elisha,	.	583
Lockwood, Mary Esther,	.	512
" Sarah,	.	391
Lord, Hannah,	.	122
Losee, Julia,	.	478
Louis XVI., Page 6.		
Lounsbury, Georgiana,	.	340
Love, Peter,	.	112
" Zephaniah,	.	525
Lyon, Moses,	.	151
MacKinnon, John,	.	194
MacMahon, de, Christine Pauline,		
Charlotte, Page 7.		
Mallette, Emeline,	.	365
Mallory, Betsey,	.	70
" Nathan,	.	70
Mann, Matilda,	.	251
Maricle, Levi,	.	570
Marsh, Charles Sherman,	.	354
Martin, Mary,	.	372
" Mary Elizabeth,	.	213
Martyn, Elizabeth Ellen,	.	384
Marvin, Timothy,	.	156
Matthews, Delia Ann,	.	274
Maxon, Erasmus Darwin,	.	305
Mayo, Zelotes Bingham,	.	559
McCuen, Joseph,	.	301
McDonald, Anna,	.	25
" Willis,	.	379
McFarland, Robert,	.	281
McKee, Sarah,	.	490
Mead, Amos,	.	393
" Cyrus,	.	389
" Cyrus Alanson,	.	392
" Elvin,	.	201
" Franklin,	.	398
" Harriet,	.	387
" Horace Dewey,	.	399
" Israel Dewey,	.	396
" Joseph,	.	78
" Lewis,	.	391
" Lyman,	.	388
" Lyman,	.	397
" Matthew, Page 20.		
" Phylinda,	.	394

Mead, Sarah Ann,	. . .	400
" Sophronia,	. .	395
" Thaddeus, Page 14.		
" Thomas,	. . .	78
" Wakeman,	. .	390
Meaker, Eunice,	. .	39
" Jared,	. .	39
Merrell, Josephine E.,	.	517
Merriam, Betsey,	. .	184
Merrick, Lester,	. .	224
" Hiram,	. .	219
Mervine, Matthew, Page 20.		
Miles, Sarah,	. .	31
" Stephen,	. .	31
Miller, Dr. A. P., Page 42.		
" David,	. .	43
" Henry, Page 42.		
" John,	. .	82
" Joseph,	. .	328
" Justus,	. .	587
" Mary,	. .	82
" Nabby Ann,	. .	213
" Nabby Pickering,	.	43
Mitchell, Harriet Louisa,	.	559
" Lovell Aramel,	.	557
" Norman Norton,	.	560
" Robert,	. .	124
" William Henry Harrison,	. .	558
Monroe, David,	. .	15
" Mary,	. .	15
Monson, Alfred Patten,	.	480
Montange, Lotitia,	. .	574
Moore, Maria,	. .	304
Morey, Almira,	. .	59
Morgan, Emily,	. .	339
Morris, Mary, Page 24.		
" Roger, Page 24.		
Morrison, John,	. .	441
Morse, Abigail Dudley,	.	153
Murray, Jane,	. .	391
Mygatt, Clarissa Ruth,	.	513
" Comfort Starr,	..	477
" Eli,	. .	103
" Eli,	. .	474
" George,	. .	479
" Harriet Augusta,	.	480
" Henry Thomas,	.	478
Mygatt, Jane Ann,	. .	475
" John Eli,	. .	473
" John Peck,	. .	476
" Joseph,	. .	103
" Martha Downs,	.	513
" William Judson,	.	472
Nash, Catharine,	. .	459
Neill, Mark,	. .	553
Nelson, James,	. .	261
Nichols, Abraham Resseguie,	.	117
" Abram R.,	. .	536
" Anna Maria,	.	545
" Annis,	. .	112
" Betsey Hubbell,	.	440
" Caroline B.,	.	538
" Catharine Maria,	.	519
" Charles Harvey,	.	547
" Clarissa,	. .	115
" David,	. .	73
" Eunice Rosetta,	.	339
" George Sherman,	.	360
" Hannah,	. .	113
" Hannah Subrina,	.	535
" Harry,	. .	116
" Harvey Resseguie,	.	121
" Harriett,	. .	363
" Helen Mar,	. .	534
" Henry,	. .	114
" Horatio Nelson Rice,	.	537
" Huldah,	. .	543
" Jesse,	. .	20
" Jesse,	. .	94
" Jesse,	. .	438
" Joel,	. .	93
" Lucinda,	. .	111
" Lucinda Jane,	.	532
" Luman,	. .	439
" Maria Jennings,	.	441
" Mary Jane,	. .	544
" Matilda,	. .	120
" Matilda,	. .	546
" Matilda,	. .	530
" Melissa,	. .	531
" Morilda,	. .	533
" Nancy,	. .	541
" Polly,	. .	119
" Rhoda Almeda,	.	540

Nichols, Rufus Hess,	.	518
" Sally,	.	95
" Sally Ann,	.	362
" Samuel,	.	24
" Samuel,	.	110
" Samuel,	.	529
" William,	.	118
" William,	.	359
" William Thornton,	.	442
" William Wallace,	.	542
Noble, Amanda M.,	.	523
" John, Page 64.		
Northrop, Mehitable,	.	96
" Polly,	.	585
" Sophia,	.	474
" Thomas,	.	457
Norton, Jerusha,	.	297
Ogden, Jesse, Page 20.		
Olney, Rosina,	.	561
Olmstead, John Munson,	.	165
" Julia,	.	586
Olmsted, James, Page 12.		
- " James, Jr., Page 20.		
" Samuel, Pages 14–19.		
" Silas, Page 20.		
Onion, William, Jr.,	.	539
Osborn, Elizabeth,	.	471
" William Berkley,	.	376
Osborne, Polly,	.	359
Palmer, Augusta Lorinda,	.	423
" Emeline Amelia,	.	422
" Harriet,	.	421
" John,	.	417
" Lewis Resseguie,	.	416
" Lyman,	.	420
" Mary,	.	424
" Nelly,	.	418
" Phebe,	.	419
" Sally Ann,	.	415
" Thomas,	.	84
" Velitta,	.	296
" William,	.	84
" William,	.	425
Parley, Peter, Page 81.		
Parmalee, George Edward,	.	177
Parsons, Walter,	.	593

Patchin, Suse,	.	32
Patrick, Charles L.,	.	325
" Semantha,	.	200
" Susannah,	.	13
Peck, Adeline Augusta,	.	491
" Alexander Gregory,	.	490
" Angeline Amanda,	.	492
" Caroline Augusta,	.	501
" Edward Augustus,	.	489
" Emily Prince,	.	488
" Frederick Silsbee,	.	504
" Hannah,	.	101
" Hannah Gregory,	.	494
" Harriet Resseguie,	.	495
" John,	.	22
" John Morris,	.	104
" John Morris,	.	481
" Julia Ann,	.	502
" Julia Augusta,	.	503
" Lucy Amelia,	.	498
" Margaret Sage,	.	499
" Mary Elizabeth,	.	497
" Mary Silsbee,	.	483
" Rachel Resseguie,	.	102
" Rebecca Ann,	.	485
" Rebeckah,	.	103
" Sarah Maria,	.	487
" Sarah Rebecca,	.	496
" Thomas Resseguie,	.	105
" Thomas Resseguie,	.	482
" Thomas Resseguie,	.	484
" Thomas Resseguie,	.	500
Peckham, William Nash,	.	256
Peiret, Rev. Pierre, Page 11.		
Penfield, Major Gay,	.	247
Perce, Isaac, Page 24.		
Perry, Hamilton,	.	544
Persons, Isaac, Jr.,	.	419
Phelps, Abigail Melissa,	.	453
" Addison,	.	125
" Amanzo,	.	455
" Asa,	.	95
" Asa,	.	451
" Austin,	.	561
" Bradford,	.	446
" Electa,	.	443
" Harriet,	.	449
" Hiram,	.	447

Phelps, James,	. . .	125
" James Harvey,	. .	564
" Jason,	. . .	448
" Jesse,	. . .	452
" Joel,	. . .	450
" Lovisa,	. . .	563
" Lucinda,	. . .	445
" Phœbe Louisa,	. .	565
" Othniel,	. . .	454
" Rhoda Selina,	. .	456
" Sally,	. . .	444
" William Addison,	. .	562
Philipse, Frederick, Page 24.		
" Philip, Page 24.		
" Adolph, Page 24.		
Phillips, Joel Hayden,	. .	319
Pickering, Elsie,	. . .	43
" Jotham,	. .	43
Piser, Eve,	. . . .	126
Pitcher, Anna Elizabeth,	. .	537
Pixley, Maria A.,	. .	367
" Polly,	. . .	80
Platt, Martha Ann,	. .	507
Pompadour, Madame de, Page 6.		
Poole, Edward,	. . .	191
Powers, Maria,	. . .	154
Pray, John,	. . . .	526
Prime, Asa,	. . . .	23
" Asa,	. . . .	109
" Almon Hezekiah,	. .	517
" Esther Cordelia,	. .	516
" Jane,	. . .	108
" Phebe,	. . .	107
" Phebe Maria,	. .	505
" Royal Treadwell,	. .	515
" William,	. . .	23
" William,	. . .	106
" William Isaac,	. .	506
Proctor, Wilson Alvin,	. .	185
Pudney, James,	. . .	82
Puységur, de, Angelique, Louise de Chastenet, Page 6.		
" de, Count, Page 6.		
Pynckney, Catharine,	. .	388
Quick, Thaddeus Smith,	. .	363
Rand, Elvira,	. . .	360

Randall, David,	. . .	118
" Nancy,	. . .	118
Ranney, David Gardner,	.	496
Raymond, George, Jr.,	.	236
" Jacob,	. .	121
" Nancy Ann,	.	121
Reed, Rebecca,	. . .	104
Renoud, Frederick S.,	.	363
" John Warren,	.	374
Ressegieu, Agnes Ellen,	.	572
" Anna,	. .	575
" David Washington,	.	573
" Eliza Abigail,	.	571
" Eveline,	. .	570
" George Fox,	.	574
" Jacob Anthony,	.	567
" James,	. .	569
" John Henry,	.	566
" Lucinda,	. .	576
" Mary Catharine,	.	568
Resseguie, Aaron,	. .	85
" Aaron,	. .	212
" Abigail,	. .	20
" Abigail,	. .	55
" Abijah,	. .	28
" Abijah,	. .	134
" Abraham,	. .	5
" Abraham,	. .	19
" Abraham,	. .	83
" Abraham,	. .	90
" Addison,	. .	414
" Alfred,	. .	427
" Alexander,	.	1
" Alexander,	.	2
" Alexander,	.	11
" Alexander,	.	12
" Alexander,	.	29
" Alexander,	.	39
" Alexander,	.	63
" Alexander,	.	136
" Alexander,	.	184
" Alexander,	.	205
" Alexander,	.	330
" Alexander Case,	.	297
" Alpheus Alonzo,	.	186
" Alvira Antoinette,	.	434
" Ann,	. .	191
" Anna,	. .	124

Resseguie, Anne,	. . .	594
" Belden,	. . .	48
" Belden,	. . .	67
" Belden,	. . .	197
" Belden,	. . .	320
" Belden,	. . .	332
" Betsey,	. . .	51
" Betsey,	. . .	132
" Betsey,	. . .	408
" Betsey Elizabeth,	. . .	208
" Caroline Amelia,	. . .	258
" Charles,	. . .	64
" Charles Edwin,	. . .	272
" Charles Edwin,	. . .	313
" Charles Lester,	. . .	329
" Charlotte,	. . .	194
" Chloe,	. . .	47
" Cordelia,	. . .	322
" Cordelia Ann,	. . .	277
" Cynthia,	. . .	210
" Dan,	. . .	549
" Daniel,	. . .	15
" Daniel,	. . .	62
" Daniel,	. . .	315
" Daniel,	. . .	318
" Daniel Meaker,	. . .	175
" David,	. . .	58
" David,	. . .	181
" David,	. . .	323
" Deborah,	. . .	201
" Eleanor,	. . .	437
" Eliza,	. . .	137
" Eliza Angeline,	. . .	261
" Elizabeth,	. . .	127
" Elizabeth,	. . .	177
" Elizabeth,	. . .	331
" Ellen,	. . .	78
" Ellen Eliza,	. . .	280
" Emeline,	. . .	403
" Emily Amanda,	. . .	256
" Ephraim,	. . .	552
" Esther,	. . .	37
" Esther,	. . .	60
" Esther,	. . .	176
" Esther,	. . .	319
" Eunice Maria,	. . .	182
" Fidelia,	. . .	328
" Fitch Patrick,	. . .	211
Resseguie, Franklin,	. . .	398
" Gaylord,	. . .	68
" George,	. . .	251
" George Fordice,	. . .	187
" George Mortimer,	. . .	436
" Hannah,	. . .	24
" Hannah,	. . .	30
" Hannah,	. . .	301
" Hannah Mariah,	. . .	61
" Hannah Mary,	. . .	273
" Harley Leete,	. . .	257
" Harrison,	. . .	214
" Harry,	. . .	180
" Harvey,	. . .	401
" Helen Mar,	. . .	262
" Henry Clay,	. . .	259
" Hiram,	. . .	300
" Hiram,	. . .	402
" Hiram Gardner,	. . .	404
" Horace Dewey,	. . .	399
" Isaac,	. . .	6
" Isaac,	. . .	80
" Isaac,	. . .	196
" Isaac,	. . .	239
" Isaac Teller,	. . .	431
" Israel Dewey,	. . .	396
" Jacob,	. . .	7
" Jacob,	. . .	27
" Jacob,	. . .	66
" James,	. . .	4
" James,	. . .	17
" James,	. . .	49
" James,	. . .	82
" James,	. . .	411
" James Birney,	. . .	317
" James Monroe,	. . .	263
" Jane,	. . .	21
" Jane,	. . .	91
" Jane,	. . .	410
" Jerome,	. . .	327
" Jesse,	. . .	207
" Joel,	. . .	54
" Joel Delos,	. . .	279
" John,	. . .	25
" John,	. . .	50
" John,	. . .	126
" John,	. . .	179
" John,	. . .	189

INDEX

Resseguie, John,	. . .	296
" John,	. . .	550
" John Brown,	. .	326
" John Dempster,	.	275
" John Stephens,	.	428
" Julia Ann,	. .	183
" Laura,	. . .	199
" Levina,	. . .	254
" Lewis,	. . .	138
" Lewis,	. . .	213
" Loretta,	. . .	252
" Lovina,	. . .	413
" Lucy Ann,	. .	316
" Lyman,	. . .	77
" Lyman,	. . .	190
" Lyman,	. . .	397
" Malinda,	. .	206
" Margaret,	. .	10
" Margaret Ann,	.	278
" Maria,	. . .	295
" Maria Emily,	. .	255
" Marion,	. .	335
" Mary,	. . .	16
" Mary,	. . .	26
" Mary,	. . .	57
" Mary,	. . .	59
" Mary,	. . .	123
" Mary,	. . .	202
" Mary,	. . .	299
" Mary,	. . .	312
" Mary,	. . .	406
" Mary,	. . .	412
" Mary Adaline,	.	260
" Mary Amelia,	.	195
" Mary Ann,	. .	551
" Mary Dean,	. .	429
" Mary Eliza,	. .	435
" Mary Elizabeth,	.	281
" Mary Emily,	. .	324
" Melissa,	. .	198
" Minerva,	. .	69
" Minerva,	. .	325
" Miranda,	. .	294
" Nabby,	. . .	178
" Nathaniel,	. .	122
" Nelson Manley,		216
" Noah,	.	42
" Noah,		56
Resseguie, Noah,	. . .	192
" Noah,	. . .	203
" Orville,	. . .	311
" Oscar,	. . .	430
" Permelia,	. .	185
" Peter,	. . .	3
" Phebe,	. . .	23
" Phœbe,	. . .	125
" Polly,	. . .	84
" Rachael,	. .	22
" Ralph,	. . .	135
" Richard Watson,	.	274
" Rufus,	. . .	298
" Sally,	. . .	81
" Samuel,	. . .	43
" Samuel,	. . .	65
" Samuel,	. . .	92
" Samuel,	. . .	133
" Samuel,	. . .	200
" Samuel,	. . .	321
" Samuel,	. . .	334
" Samuel Platt,	.	314
" Sarah,	. . .	8
" Sarah,	. . .	9
" Sarah,	. . .	18
" Sarah,	. . .	44
" Sarah,	. . .	209
" Sarah,	. . .	409
" Sarah Ann,	. .	400
" Sarah Jane,	. .	405
" Sarah Jane,	. .	433
" Seth,	. . .	79
" Smith,	. . .	432
" Sophronia,	. .	395
" Sophronia,	. .	407
" Stephen,	. .	41
" Stephen Hubbard Wakeman,	.	333
" Susan,	. . .	45
" Susan,	. . .	188
" Susan,	. . .	350
" Thankful,	. .	38
" Thankful,	. .	46
" Timothy,	. .	14
" Timothy,	. .	53
" Timothy,	. .	276
" William,	. .	13
" William,	. .	40

Resseguie, William,	. . .	52
" William,	. . .	193
" William,	. . .	204
" William,	. . .	215
" William,	. . .	253
" William David,	. . .	89
" William Forster,	. . .	426
Resseguier, de, Albert, Page 9.		
" de, Alexandre,	. . .	1
" de, Bernard Marie, Page 7.		
" de, Clement Ignace, Page 6.		
" de, Dominique, Page 5.		
" de, Jean, Page 6.		
" de, Jeanne, Page 11.		
" de, Louis Elizabeth, Emanuel, Page 6.		
" de, Susanne, Page 11.		
Reynolds, Mary,	. . .	42
Rice, Billings Robinson,	. . .	520
" Ellen Paris,	. . .	479
" Harry Nichols,	. . .	521
" Horatio,	. . .	522
" Maria Hannah,	. . .	524
" Moses,	. . .	111
" Warren Moses,	. . .	523
Riford, Orlinda Adnelro,	. . .	184
Riggs, Alfred,	. . .	152
" Alfred,	. . .	160
" Alta,	. . .	140
" Ann,	. . .	141
" Eli,	. . .	158
" Elijah Belden,	. . .	147
" Emeline,	. . .	161
" Esther,	. . .	10
" Esther,	. . .	36
" Frances Emeline,	. . .	167
" George,	. . .	154
" Hannah Margaret,	. . .	163
" Hannah Margaret,	. . .	165
" Hiram Timothy,	. . .	168
" Horace Alexander,	. . .	153
" Ira,	. . .	33
" Ira,	. . .	148
" Isaac,	. . .	145
" James,	. . .	10
" James,	. . .	31
Riggs, James,	. . .	166
" James Wooster,	. . .	143
" Jonathan,	. . .	10
" John Weed,	. . .	159
" John Woodward,	. . .	10
" Joseph,	. . .	10
" Joseph,	. . .	162
" Joseph Miles,	. . .	142
" Julia,	. . .	10
" Laura,	. . .	151
" Laura Candace,	. . .	146
" Lewis,	. . .	149
" Margaret Hannah,	. . .	164
" Marilda Susan,	. . .	155
" Matilda,	. . .	156
" Miles,	. . .	10
" Miles,	. . .	32
" Minerva,	. . .	157
" Phebe Margaret,	. . .	144
" Sarah,	. . .	35
" Stephen,	. . .	139
" Timothy,	. . .	34
" William Henry,	. . .	169
" Zenas,	. . .	150
Robespierre, de, Maximilien Marie Isidore, Page 7.		
Robinson, Bethia,	. . .	238
" Beverly, Page 24.		
" David,	. . .	237
" Ebenezer,	. . .	46
" Ebenezer,	. . .	242
" Isaiah,	. . .	83
" Lovina,	. . .	83
" Lucy,	. . .	236
" Mary,	. . .	196
" Mary,	. . .	239
" Morris,	. . .	240
" Rosella,	. . .	243
" Sarah,	. . .	241
" Susan,	. . .	235
" Susannah, Page 24.		
Rockwell, Joseph, Jr., Page 20.		
" Thankful,	. . .	78
Roff, James Henry,	. . .	538
Rogers, Mary M.,	. . .	300
Romer, Esther,	. . .	160
Root, Jacob T.,	. . .	532
Rossier, Catharine,	. . .	528

INDEX.

Rowland, David, Page 19.
Rowley, Sarah, . . . 51
Rozell, William, . . . 188
Rumsey, Sarah, . . . 17
Runnells, Anna, . . . 64
Rusky, Noah, . . . 192
Russegue, Alpheus Alonzo, . 186
Russica, Isaiah, . . . 6
" Sarah, . . . 6
" Simon, . . . 6

Salisbury, Clark, . . . 171
Sanford, Anna, . . . 121
Sawyer, Albert Franklin, . 494
Scott, Charles, . . . 60
Scribner, Mollie, . . . 76
Scriven, Amanda Melinda, . 246
Secor, Catharine, . . . 40
Selleck, Henry Stanton, . 381
Seymour, Horace A., . . 175
" Matthew, Page 12.
" Nancy Celestia, . 153
Shannon, William, . . 533
Shattuck, Thomas M., . 260
Shears, Mary, . . . 326
Sheldon, Betsey, . . . 180
" Clara, . . . 439
" Emeline, . . . 179
" Oliver Houghton, . 413
Sherman, Mary, . . . 311
Sherwood, Elizabeth, . . 43
Short, Francis, . . . 232
" Laurette, . . . 225
" Mary Lizette, . . 231
Signor, Augustus, . . . 324
" Elvira, . . . 320
Sigourney, André, Page 11.
Silsbee, Rebecca, . . . 104
" Samuel, . . . 104
" Sarah, . . . 105
Simmons, Patience, . . 58
Sisson, Hannah, . . . 344
Smith, Abigail, . . . 97
" Anna, . . . 98
" Charles, . . . 539
" Horace Kellogg, . 540
" Joseph Chester, . 538
" Julia Elizabeth, . 467

Smith, Maryette F., . . 399
" Nathan, . . . 21
" Nathan, . . . 100
" Nathan, . . . 468
" Polly, . . . 96
" Rhoda, . . . 116
" Sally, . . . 99
" Samuel, Page 14.
" Samuel, . . . 21
" Sarah, . . . 267
Soules, Mary Eunice, . . 158
Spencer, Julia, . . . 229
" Sally Ann, . . 233
Sprague, Lydia, . . . 65
Starks, George Washington, . 210
Stephens, Abner, . . . 55
" Abner, . . . 286
" Betsey Maria, . 288
" Caroline Amanda, . 287
" Cornelia, . . 290
" James Alexander, . 283
" Joel Resseguie, . 282
" John Chase, . 289
" John Squire, . 55
" Justus, . . . 285
" Mary Jane, . . 284
Sterling, Eliza, . . . 72
" Thaddeus, . . 72
Stevens, Daniel Forward, . 370
" Frances Mary, . 350
" Mary, . . . 367
Stewart, Sara, . . . 93
Stilson, Abiah, . . . 108
St. John, Joseph, Page 12.
" Matthias, Page 12.
" Samuel, Page 11.
Stone, Clark, . . . 40
" Minerva, . . . 139
Storms, Catharine, . . 118
Stout, Nathaniel Robinson, . 488
Strong, Bede Ellen, . . 521
" Jacob Lane, . . 565
Sturges, Abby Jane, . . 360
" James, . . . 74
" James, . . . 362
" Mary, . . . 74
Sutton, Gilbert, . . . 188
" Mary Ann, . . 350

Swan, Demise,	249	Vaille, Sarah Eva, . . . 385
" Elias Andrew,	250	Van Arnam, Abram Newcomb, . 337
" Elias Lee,	244	Vandenberg, Amanda A., . . 373
" Hiram Resseguie,	246	Vandeusen, Jemima, . . . 84
" Jefferson Lee,	248	Van Hoosear, Charles, . . 375
" Mary Ann,	247	Van Valin, Amos, . . . 534
" Timothy Dwight,	47	" Oliver, . . . 410
" Timothy Dwight,	245	Vosburgh, Daniel, . . . 450
Sweatman, Henrietta M.,	566	Vredenburg, Ellen, . . . 192
Sweet, Charles,	226	Vroman, James, . . . 258
Talcott, George Washington,	262	Wagner, Joseph, Jr., . . . 157
Tallmadge, Elizabeth,	420	Walker, Angeline, . . . 411
Tappan, Maria,	285	" Mary, . . . 186
Taylor, Caroline,	171	" Ruby, . . . 175
" Harry R.,	170	Wall, Elizabeth, . . . 53
" James Brisbin,	174	Ward, Huldah, . . . 49
" Minnetta,	172	Washington, George, Page 33.
" Morgan Lewis,	173	Watrous, John, Page 82.
" Phœbe,	348	Watson, James Tompkins, . 273
" Raymond,	35	" Louisa Jennette, . 561
" Suse,	32	Way, Alonzo Bigelow, . . 577
Tewksbury, Mary,	211	" Elizabeth, . . . 581
Thayer, Charlotte,	217	" George H., . . 582
Thomas, Sarah,	73	" Harriet, . . . 579
Thompson, Anna,	25	" Harvey, . . . 578
" Lovina,	82	" John Resseguie, . 580
" Samuel Thompson,	495	" Mary Elizabeth, . 584
Tibbles, Diana,	448	" Samuel, . . . 127
Tice, Alonzo,	274	" Samuel Vibber, . 127
Tinklepaugh, Maria,	110	" Sarah, . . . 583
Townsend, Melissa,	351	Weaver, Albert Gordon, . 243
Treadwell, Abiah Hull,	109	Weed, Candace, . . . 34
" Henry Resseguie,	513	" Grace, . . . 118
" Hezekiah,	108	" Hannah, . . . 34
" Hezekiah,	109	" John, . . . 34
" John Prime,	512	Wells, Joshua, Jr., . . . 294
" Phebe Lucretia,	514	Wemple, Martha, . . . 550
" Samuel,	108	Westervelt, Helen Ann, . 329
Tripp, Eliza Ann,	216	White, Mary, . . . 438
Turner, James,	242	Whitney, Caroline, . . . 224
Tuttle, David, Page 11.		" Delilah, . . . 232
Tyler, Abigail Watson,	152	" Elias, . . . 225
" Sylvenus,	304	" Elizabeth, . . . 10
		" Fitch, . . . 233
Vail, Huldah,	469	" Hannah, . . . 10
" Jemima,	93	" Jeremiah, . . . 45
Vaille, Mary Ellen,	383	" Jeremiah, . . . 223

www.ingramcontent.com/pod-product-compliance
Lightning Source LLC
Chambersburg PA
CBHW020900160426
43192CB00007B/1008